UPDATING THE MAP

A Humanist Journey through the Bible

About the author

Ben Whitney trained as a sociologist and social worker then studied theology as a post-graduate and spent a few years as a Baptist Minister. He then returned to social work and spent over 20 years in senior positions in 2 local authorities, supporting schools with attendance, child protection and pastoral care. He is the author of several specialist books for teachers and is now an Independent Education Welfare Consultant, trainer and writer. This is his third book of experimental 'humanist spirituality' published through www.ypd-books.com. He can be contacted via his website www.ben-whitney.org.uk.

UPDATING THE MAP

A Humanist Journey through the Bible

Ben Whitney

© Ben Whitney, 2012

Published by Ben Whitney

All rights reserved. Reproduction of this book by photocopying or electronic means for non-commercial purposes is permitted. Otherwise, no part of this book may be reproduced, adapted, stored in a retrieval system or transmitted by any means, electronic, mechanical, photocopying, or otherwise without the prior written permission of the author.

The rights of Ben Whitney to be identified as the author of this work have been asserted in accordance with the Copyright, Designs and Patents Act 1988.

A CIP catalogue record for this book is available from the British Library.

ISBN 978-0-9569568-3-5

Book and cover design by Clare Brayshaw

Prepared and printed by:

York Publishing Services Ltd
64 Hallfield Road
Layerthorpe
York YO31 7ZQ
Tel: 01904 431213

Website: www.yps-publishing.co.uk

Contents

Introduction 1

Part 1 GETTING OUR BEARINGS

1. Wading through the marsh: the God problem 9
2. Climbing the cliff: the Church problem 23
3. Crossing the river: the Bible problem 35

Part 2 STEPPING STONES

1. Myths 49
2. Commandments 56
3. Stories 63
4. Songs and poems 69
5. Inconvenient truths 76
6. Gospels 83
7. Signs and wonders 90
8. Meals 97
9. Journeys 104
10. Dreams and visions 111

Conclusion: Updating the map 118

'All things are full of gods'

(Thales, circa 585 BC)

'I am human, so nothing human is alien to me'.
(Publius Terentius Afer (Terence) 190-158 B.C.)

'Only thoughts which come from walking have any value'.

(Friedrich Nietzsche)

INTRODUCTION

This is the third of my books of 'humanist spirituality', alongside *'Walking Without God'* and *'Finding the Way'*, (both published in 2011 and also available through www.ypd-books.com). Those books were short and sudden; a quick and easy read, largely anecdotal. They were each written in just a few weeks and were designed to start a discussion, initially with myself and then with anyone else who might be interested, as I began to think again about issues that had lain dormant in my life for several years.

I may have a theology degree and had once been a Baptist Minister, but I had given questions of religious faith little attention in recent years while I got on with other things: family, relationships, career, watching Stoke City etc. My 'proper' job is in social work and education. In that sense I am entirely an amateur in this field; just one beggar trying to help another beggar to find some bread.

The first two books were like a series of mini-sermons, (I used to have to write two every week and no doubt they were equally rough and ready and not as well thought-through as they could have been). It seemed I still had something to say, if now to a different audience. Big human questions remain even for those who profess no religion; how do we understand suffering, morality, forgiveness and so on? Do the stories that Jesus told have any significance even if you don't believe in him as your 'Lord and Saviour' or as the 'Son of God'?

But now that I had given myself a bit more time to think about it, I clearly still had a nagging interest in the Christian church and in Jesus of Nazareth in particular. Both had been a part of me since childhood. I was also clear that I could no longer affirm faith in the existence of a supernatural God. Perhaps I had never really thought it was true as genuine believers seem to do. But neither do I think that the religious quest is entirely pointless or that the church is the wholly negative influence on society and individuals that some other humanists have maintained.

However, there are some serious issues to be addressed and, hopefully, some new ways forward to be found. We each have to decide how best to live and religions have traditionally provided a framework within which to make these choices. But so much has changed in the last 2000 years that people of faith often appear out of touch with the modern world and with people like me. To become a believer I would have let go of so much else that I know to be true, and I just cannot do it.

My general thesis is that 'spirituality' – how we understand ourselves and make sense of it all, both individually and together – is an entirely human activity, like music, art or mathematics, though nonetheless meaningful for that. But anything we say about a God is said from <u>within</u> our human understanding, not because we have temporarily encountered some 'Other Being' who is outside of ourselves. This whole journey begins from there; I can start from nowhere else.

There is no shame in not believing in a God and it certainly doesn't automatically make you a bad person. 'Secular' philosophy-based views of life have been around for almost as long as the theistic ones. For me, the much greater shame is in just accepting whatever we are told by others without question. Those for whom I am particularly hoping to write include those who just take it all for granted and don't actually know if they believe it or not, as well as those who are roughly where I am. But we all have brains and hopefully readers find what I write helpful, or at least stimulating. I ask only to be given a chance to make you think, not in any way to suggest that I have an 'answer' to offer that is any better than anyone else's.

This book is intended to be rather more substantial than the first two and aims to set out the agenda for a more developed 'humanist spirituality' in more detail. I am especially indebted to two fascinating and eminently readable books: Karen Armstrong (2007), *'The Bible; The Autobiography'* and Brian McLaren (2010), *'A New Kind of Christianity'*. Every thoughtful believer and church leader ought to read them both, but they are also of much wider interest to the rest of us. They each specifically crop up in Part 1, and are often there in the background later, even when I haven't noticed.

Karen Armstrong charts the history both of how the Bible came to be written and how it has subsequently been used, without in any way undermining its value or significance. Brian McLaren puts the teaching of Jesus, (not the later teachings of the church about Jesus), pretty much where I would put them as the church's core business. As I think about all this again, the criteria begin to blur and I even start to wonder if I might still be a Christian after all, even without a God!

However, neither are quite where I am, though both have spurred me on to new areas of reflection. Three major obstacles seem to be in my way. I keep returning to an analogy with country walking and there's a marsh, a cliff-face and a river ahead! The map no longer seems to go where I am heading. The Bible keeps mentioning a God on virtually every page and the church expects me to worship 'Him' as a living Being at 10.30 on a Sunday morning if I want to be involved. But I just don't believe 'He' is there to hear me. So I am left with the God problem and the church problem, both underpinned by the Bible problem. How (on earth) do I get round them? And what is there on the other side if I do?

This book starts with God and with the church but it is mostly about the Bible. It lies behind what Christian believers claim to be true and is the backbone of what churches do when they meet together, whatever their formal or informal liturgy. It forms a kind of bridge between the everyday and the spiritual. Or rather, I will suggest, it may be better seen as a series of stepping stones, because there are considerable gaps which still have to be negotiated if people like me are going to make any progress. But the missing bits don't necessarily mean that the whole route has to be abandoned.

Unlike other writers, (for example: A.C. Grayling (2011) *'The Good Book'*), I am not advocating that we should move on from the Bible we have inherited and create a new one that reflects a wider range of literary sources. Of course we need other ideas as well – I will draw on several – but my aim here is to look at the Bible in a different way, not to discard or replace it. And I would still like Christians, not just atheists, to hear what I have to say and to join in the conversation. I have absolutely no intention to offend, though I do have some critical questions for them to consider.

Many claims and assumptions are made about the Bible, even by those who are asking quite radical questions about both God and the church. Many of them don't stand up too well to what we now know to be true about its origins and production. Many believers who hear it read week by week, or who read it for themselves, show little or no interest in what the Bible is or where it came from, content only to quote it (in English obviously) as if that's the end of the matter. That is no longer intellectually sustainable.

My main emphasis, given my understanding of religion as an individual and corporate human activity just like any other, will be on understanding the Bible as arising directly from human experience, not from outside or beyond it. In the shelf-full of very different books that it actually is, it contains a variety of events, themes and styles of material that may help us to look again at our contemporary lives as the original writers looked at theirs. It is not a special class of 'divine' text quite unlike any other. That would miss the whole point of it. The authors wrote from and for their times; perhaps we now have to do the same in ours, not merely copy from theirs.

If you approach the Bible like that, does it enable us to find a new way to go? Can we use it to create a new map for a new spiritual journey? A map that recognises the obvious fact that we have travelled beyond the insights of our ancient forebears and now look at life very differently. Just as they would all have said that the earth was flat, or that the sun went round it, we now live with a modern 'world-view' in the light of all the things we have discovered since. That must make us question where they had reached by then, but maybe the stones still indicate the general direction. So, can I usefully negotiate the spaces between them, and without getting my feet too wet in the process?

PART 1

GETTING OUR BEARINGS

1 WADING THROUGH THE MARSH: THE GOD PROBLEM

What are we to make of the idea of a God and does what we mean have to be the same for us in our modern world as it was in ancient times? Can we find a new understanding of 'spirituality' which might enable believers and non-believers to get along better together? And even if a God is no longer involved, can we still make some sense of the Bible? Those are the questions facing me before I start. My answer to the last one in particular has to be 'yes' by the end of Part 1 or there will be no point in going any further!

Of course, for many people all these questions are equally irrelevant. God is either taken for granted, disbelieved or ignored. There doesn't seem to be much worth talking about, whichever side of the fence you are on. Maybe most of us, if stopped in the street or when we're ticking the box on the Census form, still put ourselves down as 'Christians', or at least 'C of E', but we don't really mean it. That's just what we've always said and done, like voting for the same political party as our parents did. Even my modest search for a spirituality alongside my humanism would be seen as going too far and giving the whole thing much more attention than it requires.

When I was briefly a Baptist minister I regularly used to take funerals for those who hadn't thought about God for years. Most families were instinctively 'chapel' in those former industrial and mining communities so they all came to me if no other church claimed them first! Their relatives always asked for a religious service; they probably just assumed that was what I did, even though I often gently tried to suggest alternatives. But they obviously felt completely uncomfortable and out of place there when the time came and invariably muttered their way through it in embarrassed confusion.

They probably didn't ever realise that they had a choice and could have left God out of it and done something different if they'd been brave enough. It's odd how we have embraced the idea of non-religious marriages, but not when it comes to funerals. I suppose that only reflects the rather superstitious hold that religion has at such a critical time, not a genuine belief that has been consciously chosen. We don't really think it's true but dealing with a death is not the best time to start asking awkward questions. Best to do it like it's always been done, just in case.

But, despite this residual convention, those who openly believe, and who don't mind saying so and even living by the idea, are still likely to be considered sad, mad or even dangerous to know. Religious people are OK as long as they don't actually talk about God; that's for the Jehovah Witnesses and the annoying man who shouts at me when I walk down New Street in Birmingham, not for normal people like us. Brutal though that may sound to many people of faith, that's how much many other people know or even care. Religion has become a minority activity for those who like that kind of thing, a bit like fishing; not the centre of our understanding about the way things are as it was in the past. It's harmless, but only as long as it keeps itself to itself.

The actual details of Christianity may be as obscure as Islam or Hinduism, despite our western heritage and tradition. RE may still feature in our schools – it's supposed to be compulsory – but not much seems to stick. More than one person has told me the story about the woman who went into a jeweller's for a silver cross and was asked if she wanted a plain one or one with the little man on! Looking at the world from inside the church can give a very misleading impression about the extent to which the things that matter so much to you actually influence the way things are.

Those who never go near a church may well believe in something; if probably a pretty superficial something, like a horoscope or a vague sense of the 'beyondness of things'. But it doesn't count for much in the 'real' world. Just because other people believed it in the past, or even if some believe it still, that doesn't necessarily make it true. The problem with God is that He has become entirely incidental to life. Or perhaps believers need to speak about 'Him' in a different way if anyone's going to listen anymore.

I can easily see how this doubt has arisen. I don't blame those who no longer believe in a supernatural God; I'm right there with them. We have absolutely no proof that it is true; other much more accessible ways to understand ourselves are available. That's a thought that wouldn't even have occurred to most people until about 300 years ago, but it has become the majority view, at least in our culture. Religious people have previously told us many things about the world which turned out not to be the case. Bad things have always happened to good people and the explanations, comforts and justifications that religion has traditionally provided, especially about a God-given compensation in a life after death, no longer work.

We have seen the obvious flaws in such ideas. If you think your eternal destiny is secure, it seems that can allow you to commit terrifying acts of violence – the heavenly ends apparently always justifying the destructive earthly means. And 'jam tomorrow' is no longer something we are prepared to wait for based only on someone else's promise, as people were in less sophisticated times. Neither are we likely to be impressed any longer by visions of 'hell' and what might happen to the faithless in the end. We have mostly concluded that the idea of eternal punishment is entirely the product of human perceptions and imagination, and are much healthier without it. I suspect that most religious people don't really believe it either, not, at least, for <u>their</u> loved-ones.

In addition to this scepticism about an after-life, we have also redefined our understanding about the way things are here and now. What used to be attributed to a God turned out to be caused by viruses, mental illness, human choices, movements of the earth's crust and other naturally-occurring phenomena. Almost the only place where we still speak about an 'act of God' is on the get-out clause in an insurance policy. Otherwise we have come of age, and the assumptions on which faith in a God was based no longer apply without question. Our world manages without Him, for good or ill.

In 'The Plague' by Albert Camus, which I studied as a sixth-former and which probably first set me thinking about all this over 40 years ago, there is a running argument between the priest and the doctor. Faced with the question about where all this suffering has come from, they each offer their own explanation. 'It's God's will', says the priest. 'It's the drains', counters the doctor. That just about sums up the seismic shift in our thinking that makes the world of the Bible look about as relevant as the life and faith of the Pharaohs.

Neither do you have to believe in a God in order to maintain some sense of personal morality or to seek to live well. This is a big worry to many religious people, who equate an alleged decline in moral standards with the general loss of belief and the very evident reduction in church-going. That would be fine if morality was so impressive in the past, but of course it wasn't. As recently as the 19th century, or even the 1950s, totally immoral behaviours like the abuse of women and children sat very comfortably alongside much fuller churches or a nightly epilogue on TV.

As we will see later, more religion hasn't necessarily meant better morality since at least the 8th century BC! There is certainly more <u>difference</u> in moral standards now, but that isn't necessarily the same as a decline. We may not all agree on what is right and wrong, but few people have no sense of the distinction as they personally define it. Commitment to many of our more universal values, like eradicating poverty and the human rights of the individual, is significantly higher than it used to be, and not just found in people of faith. I am afraid that Northern Ireland and the USA, where going to church still seems to be part of the national identity to a much greater extent than elsewhere, hardly provide convincing examples of its impact. Apartheid South Africa used to be the same.

We have also become more culturally diverse, as well as more intellectually aware. Christianity does not have the field all to itself anymore, so that is bound to call into question whether it is necessarily any more true than any other religion. They can't all be right about their claims for their mutually-exclusive God, so maybe none of them are. To show how open-minded I was, I used to quote the ancient images of many different paths up the same mountain or the varying convictions of the blind men who could only describe what an elephant is like from the small part of the whole that they could touch. But maybe there is no mountain. Perhaps the elephant in the room is that there is no elephant in the room!

Religion doesn't actually need a God behind it all to understand it sociologically. It makes sense as a human construct. It provides answers to real questions – or at least it used to do so before many of us began to look elsewhere. There is no part of any faith tradition that operates outside human interpretation. A religious event is a human event understood as a religious event. But it can equally be understood as something else.

I accept, of course, that the authority of a God has been the way most human beings have traditionally chosen to underpin their systems of value and behaviour, at least until relatively recently. This may make it all sound beyond dispute. But such an idea is still all our own doing, largely arising from the need for personal meaning or from a deliberate desire to impose social order and control over others. So, for all the time I have spent recently in thinking and writing about 'Him', I would still have to regard the idea of a supernatural God as a human projection; an external personalisation of our spiritual quest, not the source of it.

So do we need a new kind of religion that works without a God? A writer like Alain de Botton, ('*Religion for Atheists*' (2012)), still sees a crucial place for religious-type activities, even without a God to underwrite them. He argues that the sorts of things that religion has always provided – reflection, beauty, community, examples to follow etc. – should now be found in other kinds of entirely human enterprises. But we should still draw on the historic activities of believers to help us, even if we now reject the actual beliefs. So he suggests that we need new ways in which to explore these same ideals together, and a robust attempt to educate people into new ways of living well which would use, for example, art, architecture and philosophy to extend our horizons and celebrate our humanity.

I can recognise a parallel with much that I have already written in this. But, as will be seen later, I am less positive than de Botton about the way that conventional religion does things. I am not convinced that it has so much to teach us about my kind of spirituality and his continued acceptance of the idea of a (presumably entirely human) 'soul' is somewhat puzzling. This too doesn't quite work for me. I don't think I am looking for an alternative Godless 'religion' in quite that sense, just as I am not looking for another 'Bible' to replace the one we have.

I have to accept that the Judao/Christian tradition has been highly influential in my formation as a person and cannot be entirely discarded. But I also have no choice but to remain an atheist as far as conventional believers are concerned. So can it all be re-interpreted in some meaningful way? Can I, first of all, have any more confidence in some other understandings of 'God' than I did when I started? – though this quest should in no way be interpreted as some kind of back-door theism.

These ideas also derive from human reflection alone, as all 'God-words' (theology) must do, but they may at least enable me to engage more constructively with those of a more traditional faith. And, perhaps surprisingly, it is a re-reading of the Bible that enables me to find at least some signs of this new kind of God even there. The fact is that the Bible contains a variety of understandings of God, not only one, take it or leave it.

But isn't the Bible all about an all-powerful God-Being who does massive cosmic things, so if you take Him away there can't be anything of value left? It's all about Him up there and us down here. That would be the usual response of the believer and many good people will be content to leave it at that, even though most of us are not convinced. They are, of course, entirely entitled to do so. But I am beginning to see that this is not the only picture of God to be found in the Bible. It's an evolving story, or a gradual 'revelation' in the writers' own terms. Perhaps I am much more in tune with some of the understandings that are less about a supernatural 'Action Man' and more about finding a truth about myself that enables me to be fully human.

Those of us exploring all this within the Christian tradition should always begin, and in a sense end, with Jesus of Nazareth, *Emmanuel:* 'God with us'; the human face of God. However you put it, this drives a coach and horses through the idea of a God who is a completely different order of Being. This is a God who lives and dies as a human life, not one who invades it from outside. Jesus is the human expression of God; and how can I possibly know about anything else that is outside the scope of my humanity?

This idea of God being with us cannot meaningfully be a statement that can only be true about one particular person hundreds of years ago. It is surely a paradigm of what might yet be true of us all? (This also makes Jesus' maleness unimportant as a defining characteristic of God, though it seems to be a major hang-up for some, as if their God could not possibly have become a woman). But there is no value in seeing Jesus as a complete 'one-off' who was also God. That would make him a unique specimen of 'humanity' who was entirely different in nature from everyone else; not human at all then.

This was the subject of massive and acrimonious debate among the early church Fathers. The birth stories risk this conclusion though that is probably not their intention. Some biblical texts are wrestling with complex terms in Greek which have no exact equivalent in English. We may talk about Jesus as God 'appearing in human form' or that he alone was 'without sin'. So did he just look like a proper human being but he wasn't one really? That certainly won't do. Jesus of Nazareth was as human as I am – that is non-negotiable. It's the sense in which he was also 'God' that will have to be re-defined if this idea is still going to mean anything.

We need to get away from the Platonic view that the human in some way reflects the greater reality of the divine and say in a more Aristotelian way that the divine is to be found in what's going on around us now. (See Brian McLaren for a fascinating evangelical Christian exploration of this idea and its implications). If there is a genuine kind of spirituality that suggests we can each be 'like Jesus' – and there is plenty – then that isn't saying that you too can be sent from heaven to be incarnate of the Virgin Mary and so on. It's saying that each human person, born in the entirely normal way, also contains the possibility of being 'God', as he was. We can all be the person Jesus was, and that is what 'God' is for us.

The New Testament writers say that Jesus is my brother – the first-born of a new community. 'Son of God' was a label previously given to the Old Testament kings, not a unique title. We can all be sons (and daughters) of God. Jesus of Nazareth has demonstrated that 'Godness' is part of our humanity, at least as well as a God somewhere else (in their understanding); maybe even instead of such an idea (in mine).

This is a 'God in us' not a 'God out there' and that's certainly as far as I can go. Finding this new perspective on ourselves is the goal of that inward journey of self-discovery which I occasionally combine with the aesthetic glory of a sung liturgy. I recognise that's not 'faith' as it is usually understood, so I don't join in with the Apostles' Creed when I occasionally attend my local Cathedral, and could not do so with integrity. But the experience may still offer me a glimpse into the 'God within'.

I am not going to try and defend this concept with direct biblical quotes. That would be cheating as I'm sure that none of the writers necessarily had this idea in mind. It wouldn't fit their historical context. There are hints of other kinds of understandings of God here and there: the observation by Elijah that God was in the 'still small voice', not in the earthquake, wind or fire; the more feminine and pastoral images of God such as 'Him' being like a mother hen or a shepherd, not a strutting general at the head of an army; Jesus struggling in the Garden of Gethsemane to discover his individual purpose rather than being given a direct instruction over which he had no choice.

And, of particular interest and complexity, and way beyond my full understanding, is the opening of John's Gospel which equates God, in Jesus, with the multi-faceted <u>secular</u> Greek concept of the *logos*. Again there is no exact equivalent in English, as there wasn't in Latin. It's the Vulgate Bible from which we primarily get the idea of 'the Word' because *logos* was translated as *verbum*. But *logos* can also mean 'reason' (as in 'logic'). God is in our reason; indeed, Jesus is reason 'made flesh'. Perhaps it is our capacity to reason that puts us in touch with the divine, rather than cutting us off from 'Him'. There's a thought to grapple with which I may well come back to later.

None of these images, of course, necessarily suggest that the God they are describing does not 'exist'. It's just that they are not all the same and some essentially point us inwards, not outwards. But even the more conventional descriptions of God are not only those of the powerful Mover and Shaker, or worse the Judge and Jury, both of which seem to dominate much conventional faith, at least on the surface.

It often feels like religion has offered us only the rather outdated, pre-Jesus model – a God who is different from us, not one with us. The presentation might be more slick and professional these days, but the message remains the same as it always was. God is wholly 'Other', (except when He was also Jesus of Nazareth, but that was only for a while). To many modern minds that's a stone when we asked for bread.

This distant God, far from being my brother, can appear to be no better than an angry parent – when all I have done is to grow up and move on into making a life for myself. This God is very disappointed in me and is constantly waiting for me to say sorry because I am stuck with my 'sin' and can't possibly get anything right without

Him. He seems to regard human beings as incapable of doing anything good by themselves and wants to keep them in a state of childish dependence so that He can take control of their lives. I thought faith was supposed to set you free, not exchange one kind of captivity for another.

Those who are still within the believing community will tell me that this isn't entirely fair, and they're probably right. Their God isn't really like this; He loves me and wants me to find Him. But you have to get past all the red tape first. It's still all bound up in texts, creeds, worship, doctrines and required beliefs; it's about toeing the party line not about a path of personal discovery. I suppose I could be a Quaker or just go on reflective retreats, but I quite enjoy having something more communal happening to encourage and uplift me. However, the God usually on offer just does not meet my needs. So how about a new language that begins with us, not with 'Him'?

It seems I am back again, and not for the last time, to what Jesus had to say about the kingdom, or the rule, of his God. If the Psalms allowed me to say what I am feeling for a change not just to hear what God's got to say, the parables encourage us to look around at each other for our inspiration. Human life is God's arena, not some failed experiment. Jesus rarely, if ever, drew his examples from among the religious community or even his own disciples. He told his followers to look at life and they would find his God there. I may not use the word 'God' very often in this journey, but I am still looking in the same places and for much the same things.

And it's mostly pretty low-key stuff built around interpreting the everyday as we get on with it, not a firework display. Or to put it in a way which gets us away from the idea of 'a' God: our human experience can open us up to the fullest understanding of ourselves and that's all we can ever know. What theists look for in an external verifier, I can only hope to find as a part of myself and in other people with whom I share the journey. To paraphrase, I hope inoffensively, 'In us, He lives and moves and has His being', <u>not</u> the other way round.

2 CLIMBING THE CLIFF: THE CHURCH PROBLEM

So, if I have to speak of 'God' in a different way, if I am to speak of 'Him' at all, what is my problem with the church? Not much apart from its elitism, sexism and intolerance of diversity; its moral hypocrisy, wealth and authoritarianism. Then there's the smug superiority that some of its members show towards those who don't share their faith; the fact that it so often claims to be right about everything, doesn't always tell the whole truth and is mostly interested in exercising far more power and influence over the rest of us than its numbers justify. So maybe those who start where I do should just give it up. It's for members only, like a golf club, and we don't qualify.

'What has the church ever done for us'? Well, there's the schools. We'd have no universal education system in this country if it wasn't for the churches, including their pioneering work among the urban poor in the C18-19th. And the hospitals, which grew out of roadside 'hospices' for travellers. And overseas aid and development work. And the contribution that religious art, poetry, buildings and music have made to our cultural life. And the way churches care for people who often have no-one else to turn to, run loads of charities and visit the sick and so on. 'OK, so apart from schools, hospitals, overseas aid, art, music, buildings, charities, pastoral care and so on: What has the church ever done for us'? (With apologies to the Monty Python team).

Of course it's not all bad news and there is much that is worthwhile about the Christian church. Many fine people are still part of it. But it's supposed to be all about 'good news' and it so often isn't, or that's how it seems from outside of it. It's a human institution so what else would we expect, especially given my view of where all religious activity comes from. But facing up to its own weaknesses rarely seems to be on the agenda; indeed they have often been repeatedly covered up or denied. The church is clearly flawed just as much as the rest of us, but doesn't seem to want to admit it until it is forced to do so.

So is it me or them that has the problem? I genuinely think it's time for the church to change its approach if it wants to be taken seriously. Even the evangelical wing or the new black churches don't attract anything like the numbers that they would like, especially outside the big rallies and events that often simply take people away from other churches for a while. It may look quite impressive but there will be just as many people at the NEC several times a week for a concert or comedy show. There might be plenty of people at midnight mass on Christmas Eve, but many, like me, won't darken the doors of their local church again once the decorations have come down.

The Church of England, the Roman Catholics and the Free Churches are all a shadow of what they once were. I often drive through the urban West Midlands and you can't go more than a few streets without seeing another boarded-up church or one that's now a carpet warehouse, office or Hindu temple. There cannot possibly be as many functioning churches in a generation's time as there are even now, once its current mostly older participants have died or become too frail to go.

Many Christians are understandably struggling to come to terms with this more marginalised status. But take away the privileges that the churches still have – and there are plenty – and I seriously wonder how much would be left. It just doesn't grab us anymore, especially now that we have a choice which many of those who lived before us simply didn't have. But has anybody left behind actually noticed what's going on?

The Anglican and RC parish systems are creaking at the seams – one full-time priest might have 15 or more churches to look after, many of them, especially in rural and inner city areas, with just a handful of worshippers. Without unpaid, part-time clergy and 'lay' people they could not possibly function, despite still insisting on the centrality of an ordained priesthood in their worship. It is particularly outdated to suggest that the local parish church in some way 'owns' the spiritual destiny of all those who live in a given neighbourhood, irrespective of their religion, personal faith or lack of it.

This goes back to a time when virtually everyone was baptised as a child and is obviously now an anachronism. I distinctly remember my college principal telling me to tip my induction service tea down the vicar's shirt-front when, as a new Baptist minister, I was welcomed to 'his' parish! The vicar is still given the universal 'cure of souls' to look after on the bishop's behalf, 'vicariously'. Well that's very good of him but I'd quite like to have been consulted first! It ought to be an encouragement to inclusion – it's 'our' church too then – but somehow it doesn't often work out like that.

It can easily be argued that there are just too many churches – certainly too many church buildings – to meet the needs of those who want to go to them. Maybe not everyone wants to worship at the church equivalent of Tesco, but in the end it's just like any other high street business with too many branches. More will have to go eventually because the customers have voted with their feet. Many might be suitable for other uses to reflect our changing needs, or we will just have to find a way of keeping the best of them open as spiritual, educational and cultural spaces, but for a much wider constituency.

This is far from a new idea and Alain de Botton also draws on the writings of my favourite eccentric French sociologist/philosopher, Auguste Comte (1798-1857). He explored the concept of what he called a 'religion of humanity' and proposed a country-wide network of 'secular priests', rather like modern psychotherapists, operating from local 'churches for humanity'. The whole thing, he suggested, would be financed by bankers; a class of people he thought most likely to be interested in promoting goodness! He was considered almost mad in his time but, apart from the last one, these seem like pretty sane ideas to me.

Christian writers like Brian McLaren would argue that the church has only itself to blame for its decline and needs to re-invent itself. It has moved away from the message of Jesus and turned itself into a quasi-governmental institution, seduced by the idea of political power. All empires come and go. This is where it all went wrong very early on when the Jesus story about the coming of the kingdom on earth was distorted into one about securing eternal 'salvation', controlled, naturally, by those already sure that they would receive it themselves. The church chose to stand apart from the world, and in judgement over it, not to seek its God within it. That inevitably now pushes it out to the margins.

Sadly, the current response to this threat to its future seems to be for the church to flex whatever muscles it has left, not to look more critically at itself or to become more accommodating of diversity. The over-reaction to the ruling about prayers at council meetings is a classic example. Or take the historic legacy provided in this country by church schools and weddings. This, along with funerals, is where it is desperately trying to hang on to its former glories. But it can all seem more than a little oppressive where some kind of religious 'test' has to be passed first. The church holds all the cards for once and it isn't afraid to use them!

This leads, of course, to considerable temporary deception and turning of blind eyes, just to get the right signatures on the paperwork, not to any genuine exploration of spirituality. I've worked in education for many years and I know the lengths people sometimes go to in order to get their children into a church school, often with little or no genuine basis in faith once the place has been secured. This enthusiasm gives a very false impression. It's not necessarily the religious element that motivates them at all; it's much more likely to be about class and social elitism.

Or parents may have no choice where some would like one, especially in many villages where the school linked to the parish church has an effective monopoly. It is true that some church schools are extremely inclusive, especially in inner cities; but perhaps they have had to become like that in order to survive. Maybe they should now be handed over to those of other religions for them to run?

Getting married in a church when a previous marriage has failed, whatever the reason, is still like negotiating an obstacle course. Far too much seems to depend on the views of the individual priest or minister, not the life stories and intentions of those wishing to marry there. While never-married people can claim an entitlement that bears no relation at all to what they actually believe, others can be denied it, whatever their personal faith. Perhaps the time is coming – perhaps it is already here – when the church will have to give up this somewhat judgemental approach. Whose churches are they anyway?

I've also seen the pain that can be caused by excluding people because of their sexuality. Very few churches would be willing to endorse a same-sex relationship, even between committed believers. At this point they are even allowed to be exempt from anti-discrimination legislation, unlike everyone else who would be committing an offence if they behaved in this way. That isn't 'conscience', it's just prejudice. We don't allow people to be racist just because they believe they're right. The church can look like the worst kind of self-preservation society, tied to out-of-date and widely unacceptable social attitudes and trying to punch well above its numerical weight. This all makes many people feel that they are unwanted as they are. We have to become somebody different first, or at least pretend to do so.

The Bible is at the centre of my thinking in this book and it can certainly be argued that the C21st church is almost nothing like the picture of the believing community found in the New Testament, though it's not so different from that of the Old. This strikes me as a massive irony that is usually overlooked. Jesus of Nazareth would easily recognise the Christian church of today: buildings, priests, rituals, scriptures, rules, authority, power. It's exactly the same as the Jewish version in his time; a fundamental part of the establishment. But wasn't it Jesus' intention to sweep all that away and start something new? Hasn't his church rather lost sight of that?

The newly-created New Testament church seems to have been small-scale, lay-led, communal, informal and often confused, not certain and secure; a bit blurred round the edges, at least to begin with. As I understand it, it was also often at war with itself, (so no change there!) but this was because the key debate was about its inclusivity. Was the Jesus community only for those who accepted him as their 'Lord', or, more likely at first, believed that he was the promised Messiah? Or could it also include those who were still traditional Jews and lived by the *Torah,* as well as even non-Jewish sympathisers who were regarded as pagans by the rest? How far should the new community go in accommodating those who didn't share all the first disciples' beliefs and experience?

The non-Jewish enquirers are the ones who interest me the most. There were Jewish groups, both in Jerusalem and outside Israel in the *diaspora,* who were attracting interest from 'God-fearers': (not the best title but I think we are stuck with it). These were non-Jews who may even have continued to worship other, primarily Roman gods, but who were sympathetic to the high standards of moral conduct that Judaism aimed to provide. They even had a special area of the Temple set aside for them as at least interested observers of the rituals that went on there.

The Jesus movement effectively left Jerusalem quite early on, especially after the Temple was destroyed by the Romans in 70 AD. So it seems that these good-living pagans now started to knock on the Christians' doors all around the Mediterranean. They needed a new focus for their spirituality, so could they be part of the Jesus community too? It's all there in the Acts of the Apostles and in Paul's letters, if you read between the lines. (Chapter 3 of Karen Armstrong's book is extremely good on all this).

My biggest problem with the contemporary church is finding a way in. It looks impenetrable most of the time. At least some of us who do not believe in a God still want those who do believe to share in the human journey with us. However, the Christian church, (or almost any other religious group), tends to be, by definition, exclusive. You have to want what they've got for them to be interested in you. The point of contact offered is nearly always 'come to a service', 'join an Alpha course', 'find out what we've got to teach you', never the other way round.

We are only ever invited to see things the church's way, as if there are no other valid points of view worth considering. The posters outside always suggest that I'm the one who needs to change the way I'm going or what I believe. There is often an implicit, or even explicit, criticism of everything about the 'world' that I just don't share. Surely there is much that is good – it's their God's 'kingdom' after all – couldn't we talk about that? Where are the opportunities for genuine dialogue with those who are not seeking to be enrolled in a religion but want to explore a spirituality; places in which we can share what we have to say <u>as an equal</u>? It's very hard to find them.

People of faith might even have something to learn from us. I honestly wonder if it's just a fear of the truth coming out that makes the idea so unlikely. Many church leaders feel they must keep control over what the believers hear or read, in case they decide it might just be true and it 'undermines their faith'. There is a great deal of that, from books that Christian bookshops won't stock to telling people from the pulpit what the only 'correct' view is of some moral issue or other. Leadership is one thing; indoctrination is quite another. Many churches simply do not appear to encourage the sort of open-ended exploration that my kind of journey entails, so why would I want to look there?

There's a wonderful parody of all this in the musical version of the '*Life of Brian*' – '*Not the Messiah*'. Poor Brian has been mistaken for the Messiah, which he is not. (So this is in no way intended to ridicule Jesus; he is not Jesus, that's the joke). The crowd have gathered outside his house waiting to hang upon his every word. 'Go away', says Brian. 'Think for yourselves, don't follow me'. 'Tell us what to think for ourselves' respond the crowd! (There's also a song about Brian's shoe and how easy it is to become a heretic, but that's another story).

Why aren't there more church communities where the worship is entirely optional, but where you can still feel welcome to explore ideas together as a non-believer; openly, honestly and without embarrassment or criticism? I know of one or two churches like this, but not enough. Those that have an active life that reaches far beyond the faithful, without any thought of getting anything back on a Sunday. But couldn't more offer us the opportunity to do something good together? Not for the world because we are better than it is, but with it, in it, as part of it. I would happily respect their beliefs if they would also respect mine.

I think this is probably what I should have tried to bring about years ago, and perhaps what I ought to try and do next. I was, I am, a social worker by training; a sociologist who got interested in studying theology but who was never right for church ministry. Ministry requires you to sign up to what you are supposed to be sharing; I'm not sure I ever really did that. I should have looked for a role that was less inside the tent, though I hope my own limited efforts to engage with those on the margins weren't entirely wasted. I tried living on the edge for a while but in the end the dissonance proved too great.

But despite everything, I must still care about the church or I wouldn't be bothering with all this. I know that some of those who are still part of it aren't always happy with the way it is either. But I am too much of an outsider now to change it from within. The God problem is too great and the view of the Bible that will become apparent from now on raises far too many questions for me to be counted among those who are supposed to believe it all, or at least most of it! But I'd still like us to be friends, and to work together.

So I have a word or two for the faithful here. We could begin by discussing the conclusions that I come to in the rest of this book. I'd like to know what you think and discover where there might be some common ground between us, but you'd have to be willing to read it first! I want to recruit you for a change, but I'm also asking you to do things differently.

If we are to explore a new kind of personal and corporate spirituality, I for one don't want it to look at all like the current idea of a church. For the modern world, and for modern-thinking people like me, your God and the way you go about your business have become a barrier, not an opportunity. That may sound like a failing on our part, but I and many others are not going to be convinced. We're not looking for 'answers' but we would like to discuss the questions!

I'm sure such conversations already happen in academic circles, but what about the rest of us? (See chapter 8 in Part 2 for an idea about where such encounters might take place). Can you find some new ways to talk about your God and to hear what we've got to say in response to your grand claims? Can you meet us more than half way if necessary? Because we might just be onto something about the way life is. Yours is not the only search for truth that's going on. At the moment, all we hear is an empty noise. Indeed, religious people seem far more interested in talking to their God, or to each other, than in listening to us. That is the church problem, for me at least.

3 CROSSING THE RIVER: THE BIBLE PROBLEM

The Bible has often been seen by believers as a kind of map – 'a lamp to our feet and a light to our path'. People of faith have turned to parts of it for over 2000 years. So here's the third problem: surely that must also mean that it's now well out of date? We have travelled far since the 1st century AD, let alone from 600 or more years before that. We now find ourselves in places that the Bible writers could never have imagined. And yet conventional faith says that it is more reliable as a source of ultimate truth than anything we have discovered since. I just don't think that can possibly be right.

My starting-point here is that of course, like the church, the Bible is still worth something. It would be the height of arrogance to suggest otherwise. But there are bound to have been new insights since it was written that we now have to take into account. Even the old hymn used to say 'The Lord hath yet more light and truth to break forth from His Word'. It's a work in progress; as we discover more, it needs to be updated and revised or it becomes moribund and redundant.

I was brought up on the Bible. I regularly heard it read in church as a child and learnt the stories virtually off by heart in Sunday School. Moses, Joseph, David, Mary,

Jesus, Peter, Paul; I know them all like past members of my family. My children even owe their names to two of them. Later I studied it as part of my theology degree, including getting to grips with some New Testament Greek, though, unlike my father and older brother I never tried to master Hebrew. Any language that requires you to read it from right to left across the page and from the back of the book towards the front has lost me before I even start!

I then spent several years preaching from it, often twice on a Sunday, with hours of preparation and reflection beforehand, though it probably didn't always look like that to those who had to listen to the end result. I once wrote a series of leaflets to help others to do the same; to understand the text, (exegesis) and then apply it to their lives, (hermeneutics). I am steeped in the Bible. I could answer questions on it on 'Mastermind'. It is an undeniable part of me that I can never hope, or would ever wish, to abandon.

I am generally not in tune with most modern people here. The Bible is largely unknown to them and few will have the first idea, for example, what the difference might be between the Old and New Testaments. The conventional understanding of God has increasingly been met with an indifferent shrug, and the church regarded with little more than benign tolerance. Similarly, the Bible has been relegated to historical obscurity or seen as a precious literary gem but still to be left largely unread; just a kind of fossil from a distant age. (Witness the King James Bibles foisted on all schools whether they wanted one or not and which no-one was willing to pay for!)

This change in our thinking should come as no surprise. Life moves on. We can change our understanding from what was thought to be true in the past if we want to and most people in our culture now have. Just as writing itself has evolved over more than 3000 years, so has the meaning of the words we use. The Bible has been subject to this entirely human process just like everything else.

We are now living with the insights of the scientific search for knowledge. We know that all scriptures and holy books have a historical context of time and place that we can identify and trace. Even if a God did 'breathe' the words, 'He' did it through a specific person or community. But it was all such a long time ago. Has He had nothing to say since? So we have generally discarded the Bible as having any value for our modern life. Bits linger on here and there, much like lines from Shakespeare, even if we can't remember exactly where they've come from. But most people wouldn't even realise what they are quoting when they talk about 'no peace for the wicked' or 'wheels within wheels'.

For Christians, of course, the Bible is still claimed to be central, but they are clearly the ones who are out of step. And most only read, or take much notice of, a small percentage of it, despite some who affirm that the whole thing is somehow 'God's Word'. To be fair, even they don't have much choice but to be selective. Much of the Bible seems incompatible with what else we know and a truly 'biblical' lifestyle would look very odd indeed. They too have to grapple with its antiquity, cultural anachronisms, inconsistencies, and at times even its inaccuracies, but tend not to worry too much about that or where it all came from. The important thing is that it 'speaks' to us, now.

As an outsider, I have to say that I am sometimes appalled by the cavalier way in which this is done, with little or no regard for the original setting, only for what we want it to say today. This strikes me as little more than literary opportunism. I could find plenty of other quotes in both ancient and more modern literature elsewhere, like those at the beginning of this book, which would do the job just as well. I have learnt an enormous amount from other books that I have read. Why should the Bible be more important than anything else human beings have written since?

So, to ask what might seem a rather odd question: 'Is the Bible an essentially 'religious' book at all and must it necessarily be seen in that way'? Of course it is set in a religious context, but it's actually about <u>human</u> life and what the writers saw as the significance of their God within it. As I have already suggested, the understanding of God in the Bible evolved over time as events unfolded that challenged old certainties and led to new insights. The ground of that reflection was 'real' life, this life, our life. The Bible is a series of responses to human experience, which in ancient times were formulated in the context of a developing sense of a God, but which, I suggest, can also be seen in a different way.

The Bible is not God's word to us; it's our words about God, but also about ourselves in particular times and places. Human beings wrote it, changed it and re-interpreted it; that is undeniable even by the most ardent traditionalist. It's the Gospel 'according to Matthew' etc., not 'according to God'. In other cases we don't know who the exact writers were, but nobody believes it dropped already-written from heaven.

The Bible grew out of actual events, many of which we can identify to specific times, places and people. It tells of the human story, which I'm still living. The creation of an external God was one way of interpreting those events. But maybe there are other ways to make sense of the same journey. Perhaps paying more attention to what kind of literature the Bible is and the kinds of activities it describes, can tell us just as much about ourselves as the words themselves are supposed to do.

So I would claim that I am taking the Bible extremely seriously, perhaps more seriously than treating it only as some kind of recipe book to be dipped into on demand to see what God's got to say today. As I reflect on the variety of its contents in Part 2, I will spend a lot of time talking about what kind of material it is and where it came from. Sadly such understandings are frequently ignored but just reading it tells you little about its context.

If you stay with me to the end, I guarantee that you will discover a lot more about the Bible here than you would find in many Christian books. I'm not just going to repeat what it says as if that's the end of the discussion, I'm going to investigate the kinds of things it covers and why. With some help from Karen Armstrong here and there, I am going to seek out the human perceptions *behind* how it came to be written. This should help me discover whether it still tells me anything about how to live now, even if there is no external God to help us. 'If things like this were true then, what similar things are true now'?

'The Bible' is not of course a book at all. It's a stack of books or a library, covering at least a thousand year story up to the end of the 1st century after Jesus and a huge range of contexts and reasons for being written. The books are not all of the same kind, nor necessarily all of the same lasting value. 'The Bible says' is a phrase that should never be used if we are to be faithful to those who wrote it. No-one set out to write a Bible and no one writer speaks on behalf of it all. Its individual and collective writers say different things in different places. The instructions, letters, legends, songs, memories and writings it contains only became a 'Bible' much later, in some cases much much later.

The Bible as we know it finally came about through the decisions of a committee as late as the 16th century, (though largely based on a much earlier list), who at that time had particular reasons for including, or not including, what they did. There is still no absolute agreement between the different Christian traditions over what should be included – it's been a human process all through. Earlier manuscripts were constantly changed and new bits added to meet the needs of a new situation.

And of course we only have the Bible books as later copies of what was first written; no original documents exist, only a few early fragments. Some of it never had an agreed 'first' version anyway. In the case of English, the first copies were made from translations of translations, despite the reverence with which the King James Bible is still regarded by some as somehow more 'original'. So how much can we rely on what it says?

One of my favourite days out is a trip to the British Museum, (even if nearly everything in it isn't actually British!). It's a massive treasure-trove of human history, skill and knowledge from all over the world, especially from ancient times. I have often found myself tagging onto a group of serious-looking people with 'Bible Tour' badges, constantly thumbing through their Bibles, obviously seeking to discover that what it says is 'true'; i.e. that it fits with what else we know about the same times from elsewhere.

Of course it does. The Bible is an element of our recorded human history like so many other sources, not some unique alien invader. Much of the Old Testament in particular is about 'politics', which other historical sources can equally help us to understand if we are interested in such things. But this can be a rather selective process because we may have decided in advance that the Bible must supersede all other knowledge.

A group I was following walked straight past the Flood Tablet which shows how widespread the myth of a flood was; not something confined only to early Jewish history and the direct action of its God, but borrowed from an older non-Jewish source, the Epic of Gilgamesh. There are historical problems here and there; apparently there were no walls around Jericho at the time they are supposed to have fallen down, and evidence for the scale of the Egyptian liberation is at best patchy. But the Bible is mostly an interpretation of what actually happened, not a fairy story that came out of nowhere, so there is plenty of supporting evidence available.

However, I am not so much focussed on the accuracy of what the authors wrote as on <u>why</u> they wrote it and what kind of writing it is. I cannot sit at the Bible writers' feet in order to learn directly from them about how I might live here and now – how can such a thing be possible in that simplistic sense? How can you apply their ancient Middle Eastern world to contemporary Europe? We don't do that with anything else from so long ago. It is clearly naive to suggest that the way social and moral questions were dealt with in a patriarchal, male-dominated, pre-scientific culture over 2000 years ago can tell us exactly what to do about the issues that we face today.

And what would be the point in seeking only to recreate such a past? Was their world any more successful, happy and humane than ours? It can easily be argued that the reverse is true. I see little or no value in approaching the Bible as if we were a re-enactment group pretending for an hour or two on a Sunday that we are still fighting the Civil War and trying to live as they did. Religious people, with the possible exception of the Amish, shouldn't be mistaken for some kind of historical society, though it can sometimes appear as if that's all they're interested in.

But despite the problem of antiquity, behind the Bible there is still a story of human perseverance in the face of often massive difficulties. A quest for knowledge and self-understanding born out of things like famine, conflict, injustice, national struggles and moral uncertainties. That makes it sound much more contemporary. It has constantly been used, in its own time and since, to interpret new events as they happened. Reading it is not only a religious journey; only small parts of the Bible are concerned primarily with worship and ritual in order to sustain a personal, tribal and collective identity. It's about much more than that.

The writers wrote for <u>their</u> time, not for ours. That's my point of contact. Can I build on their insights to do the same now, to rewrite and update the ancient map as a way to reflect on <u>my</u> experience? Even when they were writing long after the events they describe, or editing older material, their purpose was still to understand their life as it was for them at the time. That's what everyone has done with the text in the last two millennia.

You can never truly read the Bible without asking questions like, 'What kind of writing is this'? Why did they write it like this and who was it for'? 'What was going on in the lives of those who wrote it and read it'? That's essential to do it justice. But then we have to do even more if the Bible is to retain any place in modern thinking, at least beyond the confines of an increasingly marginalised church.

We also have to put it to work, but now in what for most of us is a secular, humanistic culture, not a theocentric one. So I'm going to look at the Bible in part chronologically, but also thematically, exploring the different kinds of human voices and experiences that it reveals. And then I'm going to look for parallels in my own world and in the contexts within which I am trying to make sense of it all, just as they did.

I approach this task in all humility, given who else has had a go! Massive books of academic theology, let alone thousands of more accessible guides, have been written about the Bible. There has been a long tradition of archaeological and historical research to help us understand the text and how it came to be written. A lot of these conclusions are widely accepted and uncontroversial except for those who refuse to listen to all reason. But I beg to suggest that it's my Bible as much as theirs and that each new generation, culture and community has to make their own response.

So I am also posing yet more questions, both to these texts and to myself, though, as ever, I'd be interested to know if they ring a bell with anyone else. I don't only want to challenge those who have settled for an intellectual laziness when it comes to the Bible – though I do want to do that. Simply reading it at face value is no longer credible. But even if we can no longer necessarily believe in the theological conclusions that the writers came to, do the questions that they asked still make sense?

Does reaching a greater understanding of the original contexts in which these things were written, also enable us to make more sense of ours? Can we then write more 'books' of the same kind about the same kinds of experiences? Because the one thing we share with those who wrote the Bible is our humanity. As I discover more about them, do I also learn something more about my own story and the human life that I too have to lead? Good questions, I'm thinking and at least enough to suggest that Part 2 is worth carrying on with. So let's see where these stepping stones lead, though I suspect that the travelling itself, not so much the destination, is still the priority.

PART 2

STEPPING STONES

1 MYTHS

The Bible begins with a whole series of 'myths', or legends. Although the stories are about what was supposed to have happened at the very beginning of recorded human history, and the earliest datable events would have been around 2000-1500BC, they were not collected together until about 400BC as part of the *Torah*. This was a climax to the process of returning the nation of Judah back to Jerusalem from exile in Babylon. This was when they needed a history and an identity and is when the Old Testament as we know it starts to become a reality.

For centuries the first five books were attributed directly to Moses, but that is much more of a statement about their genre and significance than about their actual authorship. Moses was seen as the law-giver; the person who saved the nation from slavery in Egypt and set it on its way to the promised land. Moses is an icon, not a writer. If you'd like an author, or more accurately, an editor of a variety of material from a range of different sources, the strongest candidate is Ezra. He was the civil servant/priest sent by the Persian king Cyrus to help with the rebuilding of the nation and its religious life; a kind of Ambassador for Jewish Affairs, part of a remarkably enlightened approach to empire-building.

While the elite had been away, standards had inevitably lapsed. The spiritual and political leaders needed to unite the people and help them to re-establish their sense of community. So, like Baldrick in Blackadder IV, 'How did it all start'? was an obvious question to ask. But this would be like us re-telling the stories of King Arthur today just as they looked back to Abraham etc. What could be known for certain would obviously be extremely limited and of course there were no original documents available dating back anything like that far.

We usually have a problem with the word 'myth' in that it is immediately seen as suggesting there is no truth in it. I have used the term almost in that way in my educational writing when I talk about the 'Myth of Truancy'. I mean that many of the statements made about the issue are not correct, but also that a 'mythology' has grown up which allows certain assumptions to be left virtually unchallenged. When I and much more specialist writers use 'myth' in a religious context, we don't quite mean that. It means a statement that might not be literally true, or factually accurate in a historical or scientific sense, but which nonetheless contains a truth.

So when the writers of one the stories of creation, (not the oldest one), said that the world was created in 6 'days', they didn't ever mean 6 periods of 24 hours. How could they have done? Days are defined by the rotation of the earth relative to the sun; it rises and it sets each day. But according to the story, there was light (from where?) on day 1, but there was no sun, and therefore no days, until day 4. It can't be read literally or it becomes nonsense.

This is why there is no real conflict with Darwin; it's a different kind of truth. 'Creationism' has absolutely no scientific integrity, but that doesn't necessarily mean that the whole story is rubbish.

It is true that the world as we know it came about gradually and in a generally integrated way. The compilers of the myth meant periods of time 'like days'; using an image from what they knew of the regular rhythm of life. We too use similes and metaphors in a similar way to describe things. 'Money (or love) makes the world go round'. No they don't – not literally at any rate. But we can understand the sense of what both are saying. The supporters of my favourite football team regularly sing that they are 'by far the greatest team the world has ever seen'. Obviously not factually true, but still true for them.

The early Genesis myths were designed to explain and to reinforce key elements of national and religious life, not to describe the busiest week in history. The world had order and structure, underpinned, for them, by the myth of a single creator God in contrast to the polytheistic chaos and maverick deities that were commonplace elsewhere. You can apply the same kind of analysis to all the early legends. They seek to explain both the way things are and how they could be.

The story of Adam and Eve is not therefore about 2 actual people, and we now know our human origins lie in Southern Africa not in the Middle-East, though that was an excellent candidate at the time. The names are generic titles, not those of individuals. It's a myth about a fundamental aspect of human nature, the meaning of which we will come back to later. And so on with Cain, Abel, Noah, the Tower of Babel etc. The writers are interested in the significance of what was happening in ancient days; they just don't describe it like a newspaper.

Myth in the life of Jesus of Nazareth is rather more controversial. In the 1970s some theologians tried to get the church to think of the Incarnation – the idea that God became human – as a myth. Again not as untrue, but not a statement of literal fact. If God did 'become man' in Jesus, (whatever that means), did it necessarily require his mother to be a virgin for it to happen, or was that just a way to try and explain it which we can now do without? There is no evidence that Isaiah 7 v.14 is actually about Mary, or about any particular biological virgin; it's all a later interpretation, not helped by issues of poor translation between Hebrew, Greek and Latin.

Similarly, even if it were proved that human bones found in a tomb outside Jerusalem were definitely those of Jesus, would that necessarily mean that he is not 'alive' to those who believe in him? I wouldn't say so. As is evident in the story, an empty tomb did not prove it; would an intact tomb therefore disprove it? The resurrection is a myth; but that is <u>not</u> saying the idea necessarily has no truth. The writers were trying to express the inexpressible: a sense that Jesus was still with them, despite having died. These are not the easiest ideas for believers to handle, and may appear to undermine the trustworthiness of the Bible. But the truth being communicated is not necessarily the same as the way in which it is being done. Myths open us up to deeper meanings below the surface.

So what secular 'myths' might we still need, given that this use of unifying themes is a helpful way of speaking about ourselves? I don't mean only the big world-shattering events but also the day-to-day sources of collective meaning that we can use to celebrate our humanity. What offers us a framework for our individual and corporate lives, granted that the Christian religion no longer does that for most of us?

Nationhood is clearly still one. I recently watched my local regiment march through the city where I live, returning from a tour of Afghanistan. The spontaneous applause and genuine appreciation that greeted them was testament to our shared sense of the value of what they had done, often at considerable cost. Whatever the factual rights and wrongs of that military enterprise, there was a unity in our gratitude and recognition of their bravery. A sense of local community or membership of an organisation would be other examples, binding us together in a common identity.

A while ago thousands of grown men and women applauded or stood in silence, and many even wept, in tribute to a popular football manager who had died suddenly, but who nearly all of them had never met. We are much less embarrassed about showing our feelings in public than we used to be. As with Princess Diana, the event is only partly about the individual concerned; it's not that they were perfect or that their death is any more sad than any other. But there are times when we want to stand up for something and a person becomes even greater in their meaning than in their factual reality.

Sporting events like the Olympics, even soaps and serials on TV or things like 'Children in Need' and royal weddings all provide us with the equivalent of myths which strengthen our modern individual and corporate identity. If we're talking about it at work the next day, it has already become something of a myth for us. Sudden tragic events like the abduction of Madeleine McCann or 9/11 do the same. Ordinary people with no obvious reason to do so, suddenly feel involved and want to do something in response. We discover a personal meaning within a much bigger event.

There is a risk here; we must be careful not to lapse into mere sentimentality. But such shared events, and the human responses they evoke, enable us to speak of something deeper than we often manage in our everyday lives. In particular, they can help us to find a greater sense of our shared humanity. The ancient writers needed a God to do that. I don't think we do; but we still need to find whatever it is that binds us together in making some sense of it all.

To go back again to my walking analogy, every life experience can become a milestone on the journey; a marker that speaks of something greater. Perhaps our greatest weakness is triviality; lives that are filled with nothing of any true or lasting significance. One function of religion, from ancient times, has been to raise our eyes 'heavenward'; to give our human experience a new dimension by confronting us with something or Someone greater. That metaphor no longer works for large numbers of us, but perhaps treating everything that happens as a potential source of a deeper truth within, might just help to keep our sense of adventure alive. Surface living will never help us find out who we truly are.

2 COMMANDMENTS

One of the most important purposes of any religious literature is to help those who read it to decide how to live. Life is complicated and full of individual choices about what is right and wrong. Nearly everyone, not just religious people, agrees that societies need commonly-accepted rules or there would be chaos. This was one of the main reasons why many of the books of the Bible were written. There is a good deal of overlap between the moral codes of all the major religions – at least in theory – and, I would argue, with what most of us 'instinctively' know to be best for us. Our common humanity is often enough to give us a clue, even if we have no external God to authenticate it.

The obvious place to start is the 10 Commandments, of which we have two different versions; one in Exodus 20 and another in Deuteronomy 5. Like the two creation stories, this is evidence that material was brought together from at least two separate traditions, and probably more, which had reached different understandings and even had different names for 'God'. The editors are already at work. The Commandments cannot actually come from the time of Moses, (roughly the C13th BC), but reflect the kind of settled communities that were not established until about 500 years later. These rules are for a society of stable families and smallholders living in villages and towns, not for nomadic tribes trekking across deserts.

Most of them are about not doing things, rather than about what to do, which is not particularly useful. Naturally for their context, they begin with a recognition of the authority of the One God. If you seriously want to see a return to the morality of the 10 Commandments, as many people argue, then you also have to accept their very demanding theological basis as well. They are a contract between us and a very early concept of a God and I'm not sure that many of those who advocate them always want to go that far. But they don't actually give us an awful lot to go on and leave a lot of questions unanswered.

Of course murder, theft, adultery etc. are a 'bad thing'; few would argue with that. But who will define when it's definitely a murder, or is all killing effectively prohibited because you can't always be sure of a person's motive? Is avoiding paying all your tax theft, or just clever use of accountancy? What do we actually do about the marriages that have been killed by unfaithfulness and cruelty apart from just condemning those who are responsible? A rule doesn't necessarily prevent the behaviour. And what about all the moral issues that aren't mentioned here because they weren't around at the time?

We need more help. And the Bible writers give us much more, though perhaps surprisingly, the 10 Commandments are hardly mentioned again until the teaching of Jesus. They were supplemented by thousands of other rules, regulations and interpretations, much of which fill the first few books but which we cannot seriously be expected to live by today. I could choose hundreds of examples, but I'd really rather not rely on a priest to diagnose my skin disease or see people stoned to death for blasphemy. (The 10 Commandments outlawed murder remember, but killing someone for their opinions sounds pretty close to me). It can never be as simple as just 'do what the Bible says'. New rules have always been needed for new situations.

The book of Proverbs, always worth a read and often quite entertaining, especially in a modern translation, goes into a bit more detail. Many of them can be read as useful advice in very human situations and have stood the test of time rather better than the ritualistic rules of Leviticus. It's not really doing them justice to see them only in this light; the sayings have a complex relationship with the concept of 'Wisdom' which means much more than just being wise. But there is a lot of helpful common sense among the sometimes more opaque imagery. Pride does indeed go before a fall (16 v.18), and it is certainly not a good idea to be led astray by strong drink (20 v.1). Much of our morality comes down to doing what we know is right, or at least not doing the opposite.

Centuries later Jesus of Nazareth picked up the idea of the 'golden rule' in his teaching – always treat others as you would wish to be treated by them. Better even than doing what is best for yourself, is to do what is best for other people. He didn't invent the idea; it comes from the tradition of Rabbi Hillel, his contemporary. Perhaps he was one of those under whom we are told Jesus studied before beginning his ministry. His own moral teaching certainly raised some very sharp questions, especially about those who placed more emphasis on the observance of the letter of the law rather than concentrating on its practical effects, but he was not entirely out of step with others of his time.

Quite a lot of what people often call 'Christian' morality comes from the Apostle Paul, or from later interpretations that are not in the Bible at all, including what only goes back as far as Victorian 'family values', many of which were riddled with hypocrisy and double standards. Paul, who might not actually have had very much information about what Jesus himself taught, seems very prescriptive, even intolerant, in some of his statements about the place of women or sexual conduct, for example.

But he was writing for a community that believed the end was nigh and some of what he says might be seen as emergency measures to be going on with until the arrival of the much greater crisis that he believed was just around the corner. But even with the destruction of the Jerusalem Temple, which many believed would trigger some direct intervention by the God to whom it was dedicated, this cataclysmic change to human history didn't happen. So does his advice still hold good?

The overwhelming emphasis in the New Testament is on the primacy of love as a guide for how to live. That is the 'new' commandment for Jesus, John, even Paul. Indeed the writers coined what was virtually a new Greek word – *agape* – to express what they meant. It's not the same as human romantic love; not the same as sexual love and rather more than brotherly love. Other words were available for all these concepts and they didn't use them. '*Agape love*' was a reflection of what they believed was the love of God but also turned into the best way that human beings should behave towards each other. Indeed, 'all you need is love'.

Given my thesis that religion derives from human activity alone, this quest for a higher form of love in our relationships and actions is something greatly to our collective credit. It has to underpin any kind of spirituality. It seems to me that, even allowing for the primacy they gave to their God, the Bible writers were just trying to explore the best ways of living in community together, not establishing rules for all time. In practice, sadly, love was often nowhere to be seen in the messy realities of nation-building and it frequently slipped away from its biblical place once the church got rather more turned on by the prospect of power.

But in the end only love is paramount, if you accept their insight. Of course you don't have to; we have the freedom to choose other defining values. But 'God is love', not 'God is the rules', seems to be where they reached. So people like me can affirm that love is the greatest underlying principle against which our decisions must be judged and which can inform our individual human journey. But we are all relativists now, even believers, whatever they may say. It is impossible to be absolutist about anything. (The irony in that sentence is deliberate!) If only love rules, then the rules themselves don't.

Take an example like abortion, just to be uncontroversial. To reinforce my earlier point, I don't think there is a specific biblical reference to the practice as such, though contemporary secular writers do mention it. It invariably meant death for the mother in ancient times. But here as elsewhere, modern medical procedures have confronted us with a new problem to solve. We can do it much more safely now, but should we?

I assume a traditional religious perspective would always be against it. But if you turn that into the rule, don't you end up sometimes doing the unloving thing? It is always a human tragedy; a sadness which I would always want to avoid. But is it loving to force a woman to have a child she doesn't want, that poses a major risk to her own health or that she cannot care for? Perhaps having the abortion would not be the best choice, but perhaps it would. It is an open question, depending on the particular circumstances.

Theists should be careful before they criticise the rest of us for our alleged immorality on issues like these. The Old Testament is knee-deep in the bodies of Israel's enemies, including women and children, whatever the 10 Commandments said. The Christian church's historic record is hardly much better. 50 million indigenous people were wiped out in less than half a century by the conquest of Central America. Thousands of babies still die because of a lack of population control. The supposed sacredness of every human life can hardly be based on this evidence.

I would rather ask 'What is the loving thing to do? What is the action that most expresses our humanity and care for one another', granted that no one choice is necessarily always right? That is the reality of human life; a realism which the Bible writers actually seem to demonstrate in practice. Jesus of Nazareth in particular often broke precious rules and taboos; he was renowned for it. Treating others as I would hope to be treated myself is not about telling them what to do; that's not how I would wish to be treated. I hope, whatever I decide, that I will love and be loved. That is far more important, and ultimately far more human(e).

3 STORIES

There's no denying that the Bible, especially the early books of the Old Testament, is full of cracking stories. People who say they know nothing at all about religion will usually remember at least something about David and Goliath, Joseph and his multicoloured coat, (though a better translation is probably 'wide-sleeved'), together with Moses in the bulrushes or leading his people out of Egypt. And of course there's the story of Christmas, which still has some residual connection to Mary, Joseph and the baby Jesus in most people's minds, even if they've never been near a church. We tend to associate 'stories' with early childhood; something to send them off to sleep, so it has an obvious sentimental appeal.

School nativities in particular are certainly part of our collective story-telling culture. Even an old curmudgeon like me has to suspend disbelief at this point and concede that the story has a feel-good factor about it, even if much of what we do at Christmas owes more to the pre-existing pagan festival than to the birth of Jesus which was only attached to it later. Almost everyone with children joins in, if just for a few days, whether it's hunting down the stripy tea-towel at the last minute, wiping away a tear as we jostle with other parents to get the best pictures or wondering how a lobster came to be in the stable!

I particularly remember the innkeeper who improvised by telling Joseph that of course there was no room – it was always busy at Christmas. Or the Mary who surprised the Angel Gabriel (and probably her teachers and parents), by saying that she couldn't possibly be having a baby because she hadn't 'done anyfing'! Therein indeed lies the problem with taking the whole thing literally. Out of the mouths of babes....

The Christmas story, like many of those in Genesis, Exodus and in the early histories in Chronicles and Kings, probably has a very limited basis in fact. The reconstruction of Jesus' early life, only found in Matthew, Luke and other 'infancy gospels' that didn't make it into the agreed canon, had to be done well after the event. There was no-one there to write it down at the time. The stories are obviously heavily influenced by the need to reflect the Old Testament texts and to find a reason why Jesus was born in Bethlehem as required for the Messiah, even though he actually came from Nazareth which was miles away up in Galilee.

There are problems reconciling the Roman census and King Herod to the same dates from known history and the wise men story in Matthew suggests a different venue and possibly a later time from the birth story in Luke. They are two quite independent accounts, unrelated to each other, not a continuous narrative as they are usually presented. And it doesn't actually work as 'fact'. Jesus was not 'of David's line' as the prophets had written if Joseph was not his biological father. Of course, if you regard it all as a 'myth'- a different kind of truth – none of this really matters.

But dig a little deeper into this story and it's not really very suitable for children at all, like nearly all of the Biblical stories. It is after all, as the little Mary made clear, about sex, (or the alleged lack of it) and about violence, when it comes to Herod's reaction to the news. David and Goliath is about a battle and a bloody death; Moses' exodus is set against the background of another massacre of children and then the drowning of an entire army. Or to choose some others: David had a man killed because he wanted to steal his wife; Salome 'danced' for Herod in return for the head of John the Baptist. Ultimately it's all about a crucifixion, and so on.

On reflection, I'm not sure that much of the Bible is at all appropriate as a children's story-book. There might be a common cause here. I once heard someone from the evangelical wing of the church say that there's a danger in vaccinating children with a little bit of faith because it makes sure they don't catch it properly when they grow up. Do they see any difference between the stories they hear about Jesus and the ones they hear at the pantomime? It all gets seen later as a fantasy; Santa, Peter Pan, Jesus; they're all the same, just as 'Jingle Bells' might now be called a 'carol'. Perhaps Christian parents would be better advised to stick to C.S. Lewis and let the Bible wait awhile!

The Judao/Christian tradition is not the only one to rely heavily on stories, though others too were certainly not just for children. The Greeks and the Romans had a magnificent array of tales about their rather naughty gods and how they interacted with human beings. Hinduism and Buddhism have a similarly rich tradition. We have always chosen stories as the way to keep a truth alive, without necessarily worrying too much whether they 'actually happened'. There was no real Good Samaritan, or Othello or Oliver Twist, but they all still tell us something important about ourselves.

The Bible writers understood that stories have a power; so they personalised great tribal movements into the stories of individuals: Abraham, Isaac, Jacob. They gave inspiring examples of heroism and faithfulness like Noah and Daniel. They told stories to provide examples and role-models, like the boy Samuel committing himself to serving his God and the lives of at least the better kings. In a culture that relied on oral tradition, these were then retold, each generation to the next, with no doubt some embellishment along the way, much as we look to look back to great individuals from our collective past like Nelson, Wellington, Churchill and Stanley Matthews! So what stories can we tell about our lives today, and where to look?

Personally, I wouldn't recommend looking over our shoulders so much, important though it is to know our history. In our much faster-moving context we need to concentrate more on creating our own stories and finding our own truths here and now, not trying to import them from what's gone before. That's actually what many of the Bible writers did; they wrote from their individual experience as well as looking back to the past. We live in the present; but the future is increasingly what concerns us. That's why just reading something from the Bible is often fairly meaningless in practice.

When I was at school in the 1960s, the staff regularly included heroic true-life stories in their otherwise somewhat desultory Christian assemblies. They were supposed to inspire us to grow up and become 'real' men: Douglas Bader; Captain Scott; Edmund Hillary etc. But what had they got to do with us? We were infinitely more interested in the Beatles and Marianne Faithfull! One person's fascinating story is another's total boredom.

Neither would I suggest paying too much attention to the media. The word 'gospel' means 'good news', but you won't find much of that in the Daily Mail! We much prefer bad news; stories of failure and of people who are clearly not as good as we are. A nation can hope to make itself feel better this way, especially when times are hard, by revelling in the weaknesses of others that we don't have. 'Millions of people don't riot'; '99% of children and young people are in school today or only absent with their school's permission' – not very snappy headlines. We are altogether too interested in what other people are up to. I would rather look much closer to home.

There are repeated themes in the Bible's stories that are still a part of our own lives, like triumph over adversity and people moving on from disaster to new horizons and new opportunities. Old Testament Joseph is a good example. Maybe he was a bit of a pain in constantly lecturing his brothers but sibling rivalry went a bit too far when they left him in a pit to die. But he made it good in Egypt and was eventually reconciled with his family, despite spells of imprisonment and exposure to the illicit charms of an older woman along the way. You couldn't make it up! It sounds as contemporary as 'EastEnders'.

But what can I learn from it? We each need to grow beyond our love of stories as children and work out what will carry us into mature and interdependent adulthood. Essentially, we need to be our own authors; to write our own histories. What is there about our individual and collective lives that we want to treasure now, and pass on for the future? If someone (perish the thought!) was writing the story of my life, what would there be to say? I ought to know. Our own story should be what sustains us in a culture that is often dehumanising and anonymous.

Religion used to provide a personal meaning that many cannot now embrace. So consequently there is also a danger that the vacuum that is left can make life feel pointless and our own part in it totally unimportant. Loss of faith might be interpreted as loss of value. That way lies despair, and it's not true. Our society may appear to glory only in wealth, success, celebrity, perfect health etc. – all kinds of things about other people that may be beyond our individual reach – but what really counts is the person that I am and the potential that I have.

I don't get that from a God. I get it from myself; my own unique humanity. There is no-one out there who can do that for me, no matter how much others may love, encourage and support me along the way. So let's celebrate it as best we can. Let's fill the album with photos and cover the page in excited scribbly writing before it's too late. Now. Today. It's the only way to live.

4 SONGS AND POEMS

Around the middle of the Bible the whole thing appears to go off at a tangent. The story is just getting interesting and we come across a hymn-book! Job, the Psalms, Proverbs, Ecclesiastes and the Song of Solomon even look different from the other books; much more like poetry than a narrative. But this seems only right if we are to reflect the variety of human art forms in our spirituality, not just literature. Music, song and poetry have always played a vital part in our self-expression and in forming our understanding of ourselves. Indeed I would argue that they are among our greatest human achievements and carry massive potential to aid us in any kind of spiritual journey.

'*Walking Without God*' is all based on verses from the Psalms. When I am occasionally in 'my' local Cathedral, usually for Sung Evensong, I hear them as part of the regular liturgy. Many are extremely obscure at this distance and I really wonder what other people make of them. Perhaps, like me, they are mostly enjoying the sublime music and singing. But, despite that slight inaccessibility, they are an interlude in the biblical journey that enables us to express some of our deepest feelings and I am generally glad that they are there.

I'm not so sure about the Song of Solomon (or Song of Songs). It's a love-poem, and there is plenty of entirely secular literature from the same time that is similar. It seems it was only included because a few of the ancient scholars saw it as an allegory for our relationship with God, but there's no real basis for that belief. It has also influenced the idea that the church is the 'bride of Christ'; a particularly inappropriate analogy for half the population. This may explain why church still appeals mostly to women. As men are from Mars, not Venus, maybe we need something rather different, though perhaps that also explains why, if we are to be involved at all, we prefer to be in charge!

I wrote in '*Walking Without God*' that the Psalms are where the emphasis seems to shift away from what the writers thought God has to say to us and onto what we want to say to Him. That's not the whole story, but much of this literature, like all artistic expression, gets us closer to human emotions than elsewhere. There are more obviously human voices to be heard at this point: like the questions the Psalmists keep asking, Job in his agonising over the meaning of his suffering and the domestic and practical advice of Proverbs and Ecclesiastes.

These last three are collectively known as the 'Wisdom' literature, though the idea isn't confined only to these particular books. Wisdom was not just a human characteristic, but a concept, almost a person in its own right; a third voice alongside the Law and the Prophets. The books were associated with king Solomon because the historical record suggested that the exercise of wisdom had been a feature of his reign. Who can forget the story about the dispute over who was the mother of a child in 1 Kings 3? Solomon suggested cutting the baby in two. The woman who then surrendered her own claim to prevent it happening would obviously be the real mother. Genius! Similarly the Psalms were associated with David because the histories showed him to have been a musician.

But these writings were gathered together later than this period, if in part from much older sources. They may also reflect the traditions of ancient Egypt and other neighbouring civilisations way beyond the Jewish nation. The faith journey has always been as much about assimilation from the wider world as about maintaining any unique insight. The Bible doesn't operate separately from its culture; then, since or now. The Wisdom writers are people like us, living the same kind of human life that we live, not some special class of person charged with communicating a truth that the rest of us can't grasp. I would call them 'Everyman' if that wasn't just a male image.

The individual authors are unknown; probably a whole range of people. Perhaps professional song-writers and poets attached to the Temple, or even priests in their own right. The writings were used in worship, but also in teaching – the Hebrew word is *mashal* which crops up again as part of the stylistic context for the parables of Jesus. The emphasis is mostly this-worldly, whatever the theological subtext; worldly wisdom, if with a deeper significance as well.

So there is plenty here for the non-believer to get her teeth into. And many of the writings have inspired other artistic endeavours since, from a top ten hit for Boney M, to 'Turn, turn turn' by the Byrds. It's that passage from Ecclesiastes 3 that has especially engaged my attention this time. 'For everything there is a season'. It's a whole series of poetic opposites and contrasts – no doubt there is a proper literary name for it. There is a time to weep and a time to laugh; a time to plant and a time to reap the harvest, and so on.

I have often invented new ones of my own over the years. I used to say to my children when they were little that there was a time to get dressed and a time to get undressed again, so go and get ready for bed! There is a time to score goals and a time to let the opposition score – when you're already 4-0 up! These days it's more likely to be that there is a time to stand up but also a time to sit down please so that I can see what's going on!

The range of contrasts posed by the writer is huge, dealing with almost all the human activities that still preoccupy us: life and death; love and hate; war and peace; mourning and dancing; destroying and healing. Life is rarely about a safe smooth passage down the middle, avoiding all tensions to right and left. It's much more like a small sailing boat; tacking this way and that, sometimes doing completely different things than before because our circumstances are constantly changing. As I raised briefly in my discussion on morality earlier, there are times when making one choice is entirely right, and other times when it is right to do the opposite. That seems to me like an essential insight in contrast to those who want to tell us there is only ever 'one way' to go.

The idea that there is a time to die, for example, as well as a time to be born, is a particularly complex pair of challenges facing us as individuals and as a human race. We are grappling with both rapid population growth and increased ageing at the same time, and with the moral choices posed by both infertility and the right to die with dignity. Some scarcely live at all and die long before their proper time, while others seem to live beyond it. I am immensely moved by the plight of those who want to die at a time of their own choosing, not when the body has lingered on after the person has already gone. I hope beyond all measure that this enforced existence, because that's all it often is, will not happen to me.

The theist may argue of course that these times are fixed and it's not for us to change them. It's God's time that matters, not ours. That's clearly not true; it fails to make any allowance for the randomness of things or for the impact of human freewill. There is no time for which we are pre-set, unless you believe in a very cruel God who programmes millions for a life that adds up to next to nothing. There are times when death seems right and times when it doesn't, either because life has gone on too long or because it's not gone on for long enough. It is pointless to wish to avoid death, but I hope I personally have the chance to feel that it comes at the 'right' time.

There is a time to keep hold of things, and people, and a time to let go of them. Children are the obvious example. I am immensely proud of my children but I want their achievements to reflect on them, not on me. There is a time to speak up and a time to keep silent, and, as the prayer says, a great deal of wisdom is sometimes needed in order to know when each is appropriate. Relationships don't necessarily prosper by always saying what you're thinking – and I don't just mean the best thing to do when confronted with 'does my bum look big in this?'!

Secular and humanist people are sometimes told they have no standards by which to live. As we saw earlier, one traditional role for religion is to create an external framework for living in order to avoid the confusion of not knowing what to do. Obviously that certainty is very powerful and immensely reassuring, for some at least. The only religious faiths that appear to be growing, or at least surviving, are those that provide people with the personal security of knowing they are right – from fundamentalist Christians to militant jihadists. That apparent success doesn't necessarily make the idea good for us. Wisdom suggests greater caution.

There is a time to be certain, but also a time to be open and questioning. There is a time to nail your colours to the mast, but also a time to listen to the other person's point of view. There is even a time, as the writer of Job suggests, for doubt as well as a time for faith. It seems to me unavoidable that we can never <u>know</u> ultimate truths beyond all possibility of contradiction and that those who claim to do so should be regarded with great suspicion.

I don't know whether it really is the little bit of grit in the oyster that eventually creates the pearl. But I do know that there is a time for the awkward question, the unexpected insight or the point of view that is not just outside the box but outside the warehouse! Without the irritant voice suggesting that perhaps the time has come to consider the very opposite of what we had thought was true, something very precious about us may be lost. Pause for further thought. A time to start this chapter, and a time to end it!

5 INCONVENIENT TRUTHS

I have borrowed this phrase from Al Gore and his work on the environment, but for me it gets us into a whole chunk of the Bible under the title of the 'Prophets'. Let's deal with the obvious point first. Prophecy in the Bible is not mostly about someone supposedly having some kind of mystical experience that enables them to see into the future. Even if it were, I wouldn't personally take much notice, (especially as it was almost certainly written up after the event). History, right up to the present day, is littered with those who claimed to know their God's timetable and then had to eat their words when they turned out to be wrong.

Neither do I primarily mean a prediction of what will inevitably result if, for example, we don't do more to combat global warming or reduce our reliance on finite fuels. That's a scientific hypothesis and we should listen to it if it's well-founded. A great deal of important work is being done to secure a future for our planet, or at least to find ways of dealing with the environmental changes that the human race has always had to face. But it's not the future that's my primary point of contact with the Bible writers but the present.

Most of the Biblical prophets were around during the time of the divided Kingdoms of Israel and Judah; the

9th to the 6th centuries BC. We don't know a great deal about most of them as individuals. There must have been more than one Isaiah, (perhaps 3), given the period of two hundred years or so covered by 'his' writings. I'm rather fond of Jeremiah; not actually the misery that the word has come to mean. Like others, he sometimes accompanied his words with prophetic actions, like buying a field when property prices were about to crash, as a sign of hope for the future. Hosea was the victim of an unfaithful wife and comes across, to me at least, as a very real person; Ezekiel gave us the vision of the dried-up valley of bones; a powerful metaphor for what life can become.

But my favourite has always been Amos; not least because he was very much an amateur prophet; a shepherd, not any kind of priest or religious figure. He came from the southern kingdom but, perhaps wisely, his career as a prophet was in the north, where Jereboam II was king; (793-753 B.C.) These were prosperous times for the nation; material affluence and a powerful voice in the region. They'd never had it so good, but Amos was unstinting in his emphasis on the problems that lay below the surface. Like any good public speaker he begins by slagging off the enemy and getting the crowd on his side; then just as people were beginning to think 'this guy talks a lot of sense', he turns on them. Calling the women of Samaria 'fat cows' must have gone down a storm!

It's the nation's hypocrisy which is his primary focus. The royal coffers and the holy temples might be full; the religious songs and offerings might be a constant background to the nation's life. But to Amos' God it was all just the noise of a clashing cymbal and He would really rather they shut up! Because their national and personal lives were corrupt, selfish and unjust. The rich were getting richer and the poor poorer; they were building their fancy houses and eating and drinking to their heart's content on the backs of those who actually did all the work. Amos even criticises those who couldn't wait for the shops to open so they could spend, spend, spend!

Justice and the 'right ways of living' demand something different. All their praising God was meaningless and it would end in tears. They would do well not to long for a day of judgement because it might not turn out quite as they were expecting. Faith in their God would not protect them if their lives were all wrong. Jesus of Nazareth said much the same in the parable about the sheep and the goats. There is surely a secular message here about the way we should organise ourselves? Not all human values are the same. For Amos it might have been about how much some of them offended God; I would say it's about how much they offend me!

We should be discovering what is best for us all; what is basically 'human'. Amos could see no purpose in religion if it didn't challenge the nation. We can seek to fill the churches all we want, but if the way we live now doesn't address inequalities and change things for the better, it seems we are wasting our own (and God's) time. There's surely enough of a common agenda here for the believer and the non-believer alike? In my previous books I explored many of the practical implications of trying to live life well in this way. Both are effectively about this call to 'righteousness'.

If the ancient stories were intended to light up the present from the past, the prophets told it like it was, now. I think of them as more like social commentators or investigative journalists, at least those of the more responsible kind. Lifting up stones that others wanted to leave alone; holding a mirror up to their communities and making them look at what they would rather not see. This is a tricky task to get right and, perhaps understandably, people of faith often shy away from it.

The Archbishop of Canterbury can try to give a lead in helping us to examine our nation's values. But if he is seen to criticise the government, he is likely to get his knuckles rapped; by both his own side and theirs! The Prime Minister has to approve his appointment in the first place – perhaps too many compromises are required to retain his prophetic status. Or is he just speaking for a small minority who can't really claim to be at the centre of things anymore? In which case he can easily be ignored. The Old Testament prophets had no such worries. They knew they were outsiders; often misfits and outcasts who didn't subscribe to the accepted way of living. But what they had to say, however inconvenient, seems to have had a truth that was inescapable. So maybe we too should look elsewhere.

Just as institutional religion seems no longer to be in tune with the mood of our secular culture, institutional politics looks equally out of touch. It's as difficult to get people to join a political party as it is to get them to go to church. We are reluctant to be members of anything, in part because we often feel let down by those who are supposed to be further along the road than we are. Perhaps our horizons have become more limited as affluence has made us more comfortable. Perhaps many of the certainties of the past no longer seem to work or to offer much by way of improvement so many have given up bothering to hope for anything better.

The anti-capitalism protest in the grounds of St. Paul's Cathedral certainly had an impact, not least on its staff. Such people are either benefit-scrounging, drug-taking, time-wasting layabouts in need of a good wash, or they are prophets. Perhaps it's too early to say but there is clearly a gross unfairness in the way our global financial systems operate and there are signs that the assumptions on which we have relied for the last couple of centuries might not be sustainable. The poor of Africa would say 'Join the club' – it's always been like that as far as they are concerned. I'm glad someone has got their eye on it all.

Many people are campaigning against the impact of cuts to their local jobs and services. We are promised yet more years of austerity and belt-tightening. We must all pay more and expect less in return. But some are asking if the burden is being fairly shared, or are those most likely to be affected also those who have few other sources of support to turn to? This is not just about the occasional library closure and the caricature of a politically-correct community project that no-one will miss. Some very vulnerable people rely on these services for their daily care, even for their food and shelter. You can't just take them away and expect everything to carry on regardless.

The average local government pension yields only a modest amount for most of those who pay into it, often after a lifetime of low-paid work dealing with people and their problems that the rest of us hardly know about. It's not all about over-paid 'pen-pushers'. Contrast that with some of the private-sector bonuses still going to those already on fabulous salaries, (including former senior politicians), and the voices of protest seem pretty prophetic to me. For all the talk, virtually nothing is being done to curb the excesses. The biblical standard is a constant call for fairness and justice, not for what is expedient.

I realise that the Old Testament prophets also called the people back to their God as they understood Him. I shouldn't ignore that element of Amos' challenge either, but I have to re-interpret it. For me it is a call to keep exploring my own idea of personal spirituality; to keep seeking to become a better person. Not to be cynical, complacent or morally lazy, but to keep focused especially around my response to the human Jesus who spoke frequently about this kind of thing.

But the evidence that both Jesus and the prophets were looking for was in the life of the nation as a whole, not just in what went on in the Temple. Religion is pointless unless it changes the world and, sadly, its adherents sometimes seem less than interested in this bigger picture. Spirituality is not about doing what I hope will work out best for me in the end. It's about discovering where we each fit within our corporate human responsibility for one another.

Faith is not about following a path to personal glory; to save your life you have to be prepared to give it away, said Jesus. The state of my own 'soul' should be the last thing on my mind when confronted with where the world around me is broken and unjust. Is this still an inconvenient truth that the faithful need to hear from someone on the outside? I dare to suggest so.

6 GOSPELS

How many gospels are there in the New Testament? Almost everyone with any knowledge of the Christian story at all would immediately say '4': Matthew, Mark, Luke and John; ('Bless the bed that I lie on'). Mark is the earliest one; Luke and Matthew seem to have shared a source about the life and teaching of Jesus that Mark didn't know about, (sometimes called 'Q'), as well as having individual sources of their own. These three are known as the 'synoptic' gospels because they look at things in a similar way. John was the last to be written, from what looks like a quite different tradition, using almost entirely material known only to him. They were all written within less than 100 years of Jesus' life and death, a very short time in biblical terms.

The evangelical Christian might say 'one': <u>the</u> Gospel (good news) of the New Testament is the same, no matter who's telling it. Jesus died on the cross for our sins, rose again to be with God in heaven and, through faith in him, the believer can receive the promise of eternal life. That's the most important part of the story, they would say. This gospel is not however primarily found in Mark, Matthew or Luke (and only a little bit in John). It's mostly in Romans.

Other Christians, including, for example Brian McLaren, would remind us however, that the story <u>about</u> Jesus is not the same as the story Jesus himself told. Jesus did not primarily teach that salvation was available through him or that his death would do all this. There are hints here and there, but we can never be sure how much we have the actual words of Jesus at this point, rather than a later reading back of what the early Christians now believed about him. The good news that Jesus preached was the imminent arrival of the kingdom, or the rule, of God. So we are up to 6 'gospels' now!

This good news about the kingdom was effectively lost once the Jesus movement left its Jewish roots behind and became a force to be reckoned with in the wider Gentile world. The focus shifted onto who Jesus was and what he was believed to have done by dying, not so much on what he said when he was alive. Much of the theology, (such as the doctrine of the Trinity for example), came along much later still, along with most of the contents of the various creeds. As the Christian religion evolved from the initial events, far less interest was shown in what Jesus himself taught, whether or not this was what he had intended.

So is it possible that almost the whole of Christianity is founded on a misunderstanding or even a distortion of what Jesus of Nazareth was all about? It may seem ridiculous and arrogant to suggest so. But most of the contents of an orthodox Christian faith come from centuries after the time of Jesus himself. We are extremely privileged to have been offered new insights by biblical and historical scholars over the last 150 or so years about the way things changed over time. That information was not available to those who came before us. It's just a pity that the mainstream church seems happy to ignore them and to carry on as they have always done.

As I suggested when reflecting on the church problem in Part 1, this makes quite a difference. If the gospel is all about what Jesus did, then believing in him is all that matters. The news, though I am not personally convinced that it is all that 'good', is that God is offering us a new relationship with Him through his 'Son', so obviously faith in both of them is required. If there is no God in an objective sense who has acted in Jesus to put right the barrier that allegedly exists between us, then there is nothing here for people like me to believe in and I should just walk away. But this isn't news as far as I am concerned.

There is no good news in the offer of salvation through Jesus unless you accept that you are a sinner to start with. If I am not enslaved by my sin, because that is not actually the way things are, then there is no news in telling me that I can be released from it. A sociologist might suggest that this is just another example of classic marketing. You tell people that they have a need, which they might not even realise that they have. And then you sell them a solution. Advertisers do it all the time. I never even knew that I needed to buy a whole range of male perfume and grooming products until the good people at L'Oreal told me I was worth it!

I'm not necessarily saying that the church has been deliberately deceptive, though some would go that far.

I'm just saying that there is nothing here for those of us who don't accept the basic premise, and that's why the church and its message are mostly ignored. It's not 'news' for the person who has no mortgage, and no intention of getting one, that the borrowing rate has gone up or down. It's not 'news' to the starving poor of the horn of Africa that a footballer has been transferred between clubs for £30 million.

The news has to relate to our experience if it's going to have any meaning or significance. Telling me that a God (who I don't believe exists in the usual sense), can be friends with me by overlooking my state of disobedience (which I don't believe I'm in), and that's the way I can obtain eternal life (which I neither long for nor accept is a reality), is never going to mean very much to me or to millions like me. I really don't understand why so many people of faith can't grasp this. They keep trying to sell us something we don't want or need. It's just their opinion that I should and I don't share it.

Of course I may be mistaken, but there's no point in just telling me I'm wrong. A good Christian friend of mine has told me that he too has many doubts about believing and is constantly at risk of falling off the edge of faith. But he also says that Jesus believed in God as his Father so, to take Jesus and his message seriously, he has no choice but to stick with it, for all the uncertainties. That's a fair point but at least we can still have much of his teaching in common. If the gospel is really about the message that Jesus himself seems to have been most interested in, then there is still plenty for us to talk about.

Jesus certainly expressed his gospel in terms of the kingdom of 'God'. That is inescapable and I have no intention of putting words into his mouth. But the meaning of the news he had to share, made explicit in Luke 4 v.18-19, was the difference that it would make, not where it came from. The rule of his God meant good news for the poor, release to the captives, sight for the blind and liberty for the oppressed. This news is not about having to convince people first that they need it; the poor know they are poor; the captives know they are captives etc. And even if there is no 'God' behind it all, such changes for the better in our human experience are surely worth it in themselves?

Many would of course 'spiritualise' these statements. People like me are 'spiritually' blind, poor etc. because of our lack of faith. Some would argue that this was what Jesus actually meant, given his obvious concern to liberate Jewishness from a captivity to the Law, ritual and so on that seems to have been part of his calling. His mission was to 'open their eyes' to a new kind of faith, not to change the way the world is. How ironic then that the religion that bears his name is still pretty much the same as it was then: just a new kind of institution instead.

But the 'impact' of Jesus' teaching and life, (a very contemporary word in education which makes us focus on the effects of what we do, not only on what we do), was on the actual poor, blind etc. The difference that Jesus made seems to have been self-evident to those he encountered. In the stories that he told about normal everyday life – farming, families, things getting lost and so on – his hearers found a new understanding of themselves and a clearer sense of their purpose and value there and then. It was all about discovering the sometimes hidden rule of the Father – the way things are rather than only the way they sometimes appear.

Despite the absence of a supernatural God for me, I am happy to accept that there may be clues here about how we can discover our deeper selves and uncover greater truths about our human reality. The things that Jesus said were important are still important, even if I can't accept the theology. This is why I am still attracted by the Judao/Christian story. I too want to affirm that it's high time the poor heard some good news and that those who are oppressed found freedom. There is a manifesto for a better life here that any humanist should also want to bring about.

This is not 'being a Christian'. But it might be 'being a kingdom person' as Jesus intended. It means keeping your eyes open to what's going on, not blundering through life not giving what happens a second thought. It means doing what you can to help set people free from the tyrannies that oppress us; from the slavery of abuse, drink and drugs that blight the lives of so many, to campaigning for a fair system of benefits for the poor or international human rights. It means seeking what is best for our life together, not standing in judgement over one another. It means looking for the positives in otherwise bleak situations and doing what you can to make people feel better about who they are.

This sounds like more than enough to be getting on with! I cannot say if Jesus of Nazareth would recognise this as the core of what he was all about. I do genuinely think that it is closer to his intentions than much of what the church has got up to since in looking after itself. But we can only live the life we have and respond to our experiences as we come across them on the way. Life is for living to the full and it can be lived well. If that isn't good news, then I'm not sure what is.

7 SIGNS AND WONDERS

The Bible writers frequently talk about 'miracles'. So, simple question: 'Are they true'? Complicated answer, I'm afraid, like most things in life. If we mean, 'did they happen?', then the answer is the same as for everything else. The writers weren't usually witnesses to the events they wrote about. Sometimes they wrote decades later, sometimes centuries. They weren't always interested in just describing things like reporters, so it rather depends on what credibility you give to them. But I am giving at least limited credence to most of the things they wrote about, so, yes, such events should be included as part of the picture.

If we mean 'were they miracles?', in the sense that they cannot possibly be explained except by some kind of supernatural divine intervention that broke the normal rules and which knocked people off their feet at the time, then that's an entirely different question. It also has an entirely different answer which I'm the last person to give. I don't know. I wasn't there. But even if they happened as described, such events don't really tell us anything. It still all depends on how you choose to interpret them.

But ask me 'were there signs and wonders to be found in the events they wrote about?', and I have a lot more to say. This takes us on to the significance of the events rather than just seeing them as some kind of spectacle to be admired. We tend to get bogged down in the 'miraculous' question, when it's their meaning that matters. As a rational 21st century man with a sociological education and a pretty good idea of the way the world works, I can offer an 'explanation' for quite a lot of them if that helps. I certainly plan to do that first. But the real point is 'what did they mean?' and can we see anything like them today?

It strikes me as highly dangerous to base a faith, in God or in anything else, on the fact that something happens which we can't otherwise explain. If someone from Old Testament times were to visit me today, virtually everything about my life would strike them as a 'miracle'. They would constantly be seeing evidence, in their terms, for the miraculous workings of their God, from invisible electronic wizardry to flying metal boxes in the sky. But they all have scientific explanations. We know what they didn't. No theology is required.

Or if we define a miracle as something that happens out of time, before it should as it were, then we're not really in biblical territory at all. The events weren't a wormhole from the future like in an episode of Dr Who. God didn't do something in Bible times that should have waited until it had been invented. There is always a huge risk for believers in attributing something to God because we can't explain it <u>yet</u>. That's the 'God of the gaps' and there's not much left for Him to do, now that we understand so much more than we did and which used to be put down to Him. Nothing in this kind of approach 'proves' anything as far as I am concerned.

Many of the Bible's more outstanding events do have a rational explanation available if you choose to see them that way, as I generally do of course. The Re(e)d Sea parted for Moses and destroyed the Egyptian army. Well maybe the tide came in or the ground was marshy. We have all seen the power of tsunamis, earthquakes and floods. The 'manna' from heaven could well have been some natural phenomenon; Moses found a spring for the people to drink from, and so on.

I don't see much current evidence for a God who breaks the rules of the natural world. It generally does what it routinely does. The problem with any other understanding is that there are far more examples when the 'miracle' doesn't happen. Why does this child live but not that one? A few odd exceptions that we can't explain don't actually make much difference to our overall world view and they pose very real questions about the morality of such arbitrary interventions.

What about the Gospels? I wrote in '*Finding the Way*' that Jesus seems to have played down attempts to see him as some kind of wonder-worker. He didn't want people to follow him because he could do impressive tricks. When something unexpected happened, according to the writers, he often told those concerned to keep it to themselves. That may be a literary device to explain why Jesus wasn't recognised as the Messiah at the time, but it may also suggest that this was his preferred style. The 'kingdom of God', his constant refrain, was a subtle and hidden thing, not a spectacular takeover.

And of course there are ways to explain his 'miracles', or they may just have been written up later in order to show who the writers believed he was. Don't tell me that 5000 people went into the desert all day without any food. It's just that they were too mean to share and the 'miracle' was that Jesus shamed them into doing so through the example of a small boy. Turning water into wine and raising Lazarus from the dead clearly had a primarily symbolic meaning, whatever events may lie behind the story. Chronic physical and mental illnesses can be affected by receiving love, care and acceptance when you've previously been treated as an outcast all your life. Miracles don't have to be understood supernaturally.

Jesus certainly seems to have had a power to heal; but that was nothing unusual at the time. The ability of the human body, and especially the mind, to put things right sometimes seems to confound all the odds. More traditional societies may still have something to teach us here. But the healings and so on still take place within a cultural understanding. Some of them may have struck those who saw them at the time as inexplicable. We might now know better; that has been the nature of the human journey over the centuries as more and more has been studied and understood.

So, for those of us who are not going to be convinced that the world is actually very different from how it seems, (but only very occasionally), what might we still be able to discern from these kinds of stories? They are not evidence of an external God; they are reminders that we need to be constantly on the lookout for whatever will make us more fully human. Life contains the possibility of amazing us, perhaps when we least expect it – I am happy to affirm that.

But such events normally restore the *status quo*, or bring about an improvement in our lives. They don't take us out of our human experiences, they send us back into them refreshed. If the sick are healed; even if the dead are raised back to life, they will still get ill and die again later. If the moment of liberation comes, there will be more challenges in the desert ahead. The miraculous event doesn't solve all the problems; it just gives us a fighting chance to get it right next time.

I have seen several 'miracles' in that sense. The birth of my children and grandson; the love I have received in later life when I thought that all hope of love was lost; recovery from a serious illness; the young woman I know whose life was saved by the skill of surgeons in removing her brain tumour. We've all had opportunities like these. Like most things, it's not so much about what happens as about how we make use of what happens.

An alcoholic can be marvellously healed of her addiction and then go on to live a full life, or not, as the case may be. The new chance can be given, and then be used, or not. There are moments on our journey when things change, perhaps in ways we had never expected or do not feel able to control. They can become signs, and be followed by wonders. Or they can be ignored and wasted.

My quest for a personal spirituality that does not involve an external God recognises that there is still much work to be done. Seeking 'spiritual entertainment' is not enough. Wonderfully impressive things might happen in a church, but so what? To me, the ability to write and perform sublime music is a 'miracle'. I certainly can't do it myself; its complexity is way beyond my comprehension. But after I've witnessed a perfectly-performed choral anthem, or even a piano recital that has moved me to tears but with no overtly 'religious' content, am I going to be any different than before? That's what makes it a 'miracle'. Otherwise it's all over once the moment has passed.

Being alive is a gift, whether from a God or from my parents. Either way I didn't ask for it, deserve or earn it. It just happened, like everything else. The key issue is what I'm going to do with it. Along the way there will be events that bring me up short, make me think, make me cry or make me laugh. There will be times when I am bowled over by the surprise of something, or someone. 'What next'? should be our constant response.

I have only once been in a serious car accident. The van driver was so concerned to answer his phone that he didn't notice he'd drifted onto the wrong side of the road and he hit me head-on. The first thing I knew about it was when the airbag exploded into my face. As I sat there, wondering if I still had legs and smelling the leaking petrol, I didn't see my life flashing before me. I was rather more worried about the chap outside who was offering me a cigarette!

The fact that I walked away with just minor injuries was down to chance and the prompt action of the emergency services, but mostly to the clever design of the car. No supernatural intervention was involved, though others are not so lucky. The idea that a God selects some situations to get involved in but not others, or that His actions are entirely random as He thinks fit, are both equally indefensible. But sometimes I will be confronted by signs that life is precious. I now have a new opportunity to go on exploring the wonder of it all. Better by far than an uneventful mediocrity.

8 MEALS

The Bible is packed with lunches, if you'll forgive the expression. Eating and drinking crop up far more often than might be expected from writings that are supposed to be concerned with what we usually think of as 'spiritual' matters. It is true that humankind cannot live by bread 'alone'. But neither could we exist for long without it and meals have a long tradition of personal and social significance. Food is often associated with sex, rituals, rites of passage and death, just to give four obvious examples that can be found in almost every culture. Judging by how often it's on TV, cooking, not just eating, also seems to have taken over from DIY as our latest shared 'religion'.

I suppose we had best go back to basics first: the story of Adam and Eve eating together from the 'fruit of the tree of knowledge'. This is 'just' a story; though it is better seen as a 'myth' because of its deeper meaning. It is nonsense even to suggest that the whole human race can be traced back to two actual individuals. Gradual evolution occurred all over the place. And of course the eating is a metaphor. Neither was it ever an 'apple' though I bet many people would initially argue the point if asked. As we will see later, many things assumed to be in the Bible are not actually there.

But the decision in which they shared together is one of the fundamental divisions between theists and atheists, as I tried to explore in Part 1. If there is a God as traditionally understood, conventional faith says that by this act we chose to disobey Him and tried to become like Him; a mistake for which we are each still held responsible. If there is no God, of that kind at least, that same step into self-knowledge, and the consequent ability to make moral choices, is when we ceased to be sub-human and became fully ourselves. I for one am very grateful for this ancient discovery of our full potential and we couldn't be who we are without it. It's a pretty important difference.

I am very fond of the ageing black Labrador who shares my life and worships me like a god, only very occasionally asserting his unique identity in ways he knows I do not approve of! It's touching to see his devotion, no doubt heavily influenced by making sure his food bowl is replenished and he gets taken for walks. But I wouldn't want to live like that myself. We are not the pet of a God; we never were. We are changed for the better as we 'digest' the things we have seen, done and heard and then reflect upon them. How else would we grow?

But the idea that eating has the capacity to lead us astray, or can be one of the greatest pleasures of human existence, also has a rather contemporary ring. When about a third of the world's people can't find enough to eat and many others eat to the point of self-destructive excess, the significance of the human capacity to decide how to live is still graphically illustrated by the same image.

It is indeed the fruits of our ever-developing knowledge

that have the capacity to turn us into gods, or the opposite. It's a high-risk strategy, but I don't see how we could be human otherwise. The ancient writers were trying to express why things often seemed such a struggle, but an innocent obedience with no decisions to make would not be humanity as far as I understand it.

Meals regularly seem to turn up in the biblical story at moments of crisis, decision and opportunity. Fasting appears as well of course, but it is meals that tend to be the focus when something important is happening. The Passover meal was the prelude to the Israelites escape from Egypt and still forms a central element in Jewish life. What the Jews would and would not eat marked them out as distinctive and gave them what they saw as a unique relationship with their God. There is probably an entirely practical reason behind the foods that were considered safe and those which were best avoided, especially in hot and hostile climates. But the food laws and sacrificial rituals provided a regular context within which the collective memories could be shared.

It was, at least according to 1 Kings 10, the food on Solomon's table that so impressed the Queen of Sheba. In Daniel 5, a thousand men are sharing in king Belshazzar's feast when he calls for Daniel to explain the writing on the wall that signals the imminent end of his reign. Many of the Psalms are associated with feasts and celebrations. The vision of prosperity in Psalm 23 talks of God preparing a dinner party for His people, which gave rise to the image of the 'heavenly banquet' to come. The rhythm of sowing, growth, harvest and eating appears repeatedly throughout the Old Testament.

But I am especially struck by how often meals and food appear in the story of Jesus. In John's gospel, his first public appearance is at a wedding reception. In Matthew, Mark and Luke, his critics draw attention to the fact that he and his disciples do not fast as proper Jews should. Indeed, they even pick ears of corn to eat on the Sabbath and have something of a reputation for over-indulgence. Then there's the feeding of the 5000; the meal at the house of Simon the Pharisee and the frequent references to salt, fish, wine and bread in the stories and teachings.

The life of Jesus culminates in a supper on the night before his crucifixion. Even after his death, the sense that he was still with them is made real when he is encountered over a meal with the couple who met him on the road to Emmaus. It seems that there is almost nothing more typical of Jesus than eating with his friends. So, unsurprisingly, as a result of all this, Jesus' final meal in particular has become the focus of most forms of Christian worship and liturgy. In doing this together, he was remembered to have said, they would keep both his past memory and his present reality alive.

There are one or two exceptions. My Baptist heritage was rather suspicious of the rather ritualistic elements of the Eucharist. So it put more of the emphasis on the preaching of the 'Word' and only held the 'Lord's Supper' on a more occasional basis, and in some non-conformist traditions hardly at all. I can still remember when as a child I was required to leave the room before the white cloth that covered the table at the front was removed. The idea that the 'body of Christ' was under there would have been far too much for good Baptists to stomach, but that was the rumour going round the Sunday School!

But this central focus to Christian worship also tends to re-emphasise its exclusivity. You had to be a proper church member to be allowed to participate in the communion services of my youth; they even collected a ticket from everyone who was there to keep a check on who was missing. (This must be where my professional interest in 'truancy' was born!) In other churches you can only participate if you are confirmed, or at least baptised, into that particular tradition, though there has been some relaxation more recently. But all of this suggests that the Jesus meal is for the self-chosen few and that outsiders are not welcome.

Jesus' actual meals, by contrast, seem to have included many, like Simon, who were not part of his immediate circle. Even Judas was at the last one. They were often the opportunity for him to talk with those who were otherwise on the margins and form the setting for many of the parables. We are specifically told that part of his 'crime' was that he eat with tax-gatherers and sinners; he welcomed those of doubtful morals, like the woman who anointed his feet with expensive perfume. This, Jesus said, was all a taster for the coming kingdom. God's rule would be like this; or would it?

There's a magnificent painting by Veronese in the Accademia in Venice, which was originally intended by the artist to be his version of the Last Supper. The church authorities told him to change it because the painting contained 'buffoons, drunken Germans, dwarfs and other such scurrilities', but instead he changed only the title and no more was said. Veronese was right. Jesus appears to have been a generous host, or more accurately, to have required his hosts to accept a motley crew, not just a chosen few, along with him around their table.

I wonder if this could be an answer to my church problem? The Alpha course people suggest that the first opportunity to talk about the programme should be over a proper meal, not just a mouldy biscuit and a lukewarm cup of tea. I think I'd like to pinch that idea and suggest that eating together might be a way into a more even-handed discussion with more conventional believers about the secular and humanist spirituality for which I am searching. Perhaps we will be more able to relax and treat each other as equals in that less formal setting. (Alain de Botton suggests something similar in his idea of '*agape* restaurants').

Sharing food is probably also the best way to create an opportunity for feeding our minds. It's often where I have my most stimulating conversations with friends and family, though perhaps that's just the wine talking! But meals instead of church services, (not just as a sneaky form of recruitment to get me to go to them), would be an ideal setting for contemporary conversations about life and its core values. I would be happy for Christians to be there too as long as they don't take over!

For several hundred years after the death of Jesus an *agape*-meal (or 'love feast') was the way in which the believers usually met together – until it was banned by the emerging church bureaucracy on the grounds that it encouraged an unseemly excess. There has never been a shortage of Pharisees quick to go on pointing the finger at anything that looks too 'worldly'. Whatever would they have made of Jesus? But spectacular church teas and harvest suppers still had a legendary status, at least as far as my childhood. I think they might have been onto something. More tea vicar?

9 JOURNEYS

I could have started from here. In a sense I did, as this whole enterprise is about a journey; my own 'spiritual' adventure and a journey through the Bible to see whether it still leads me anywhere. The Bible writers were constantly recording journeys; of individuals and of whole communities. No planes and cars, and a very limited whole-world view, but travel is still a frequent theme.

The more we discover about what else was going on in the ancient world at the same time, the more we have to recognise that the story of one tradition cannot be the story of the whole. There was a great deal of interplay between the nations even then, and looking outwards to those who are different, if sometimes unwillingly, is a frequent biblical theme. The rejection of a God who was only interested in 'us' was a vital discovery in making that happen. Every journey does indeed begin with the first step.

These biblical journeys often led to something entirely new. While the exiles were away in Babylon they came up against a wholly foreign culture and a very different religion. The spiritual life they developed when they came back, much more carefully thought through and far less tribal in its understanding of their God, owed its origins in part to what they had experienced while they were away. The Old Testament would not have been written as we have it without that process of risk and renewal in previously unfamiliar places.

Sometimes it seems like no-one stayed where they were for long. The ancient stories of Abraham and Moses both contain mass movements across the Middle East. The first believers in the One God were nomadic; everyone was then. Moving on was a way of life, but even when tribes and nations became more settled, they often had to up sticks and move on again. Climate change, water shortages, a sense of destiny, defeat in wars, occupation and colonisation all played a part.

Certain physical locations keep cropping up. Ironically, much of the Holy Land is still a matter of dispute with different groups claiming the same space. Many people feel they are away from where they would want to be, even though that inevitably brings them into conflict with others who may already see the same space as theirs. That's a very ancient human struggle.

Jesus of Nazareth was continually on the move. It's there twice in the birth narratives and talking while walking seem to have been two of his most frequent activities during his ministry. But first he had to leave the comfort of his home, which had apparently been settled and safe for thirty years, if he was to follow his search for the 'kingdom of God'. It seems that he had no regular home at all after that. And the pivotal event in the Gospel story is his decision to go to Jerusalem and confront both the Jewish and the Roman authorities. A maverick Galilean who'd stayed there could easily have been ignored.

Paul's travels take up half the New Testament and ultimately helped to turn the Christian faith from only a Jewish sect into a worldwide phenomenon – even if I do see that as something of a mixed blessing. Large parts of his letters to the fledgling churches are set against the context of his missionary journeys. Thomas Cook was first formed (by a Baptist) as a Christian pilgrimage and travel service. The company I use most for my own guided walks has similar origins. You can still see some of the key sites, or at least the ruins of them. Easy enough from a cruise ship; altogether more challenging 2000 years ago, but you get some sense of the distances and difficulties involved.

I am very fortunate to have travelled as much as I have. It does indeed broaden the mind. I have seen Nelson's Mandela's cell off Cape Town; the Great Wall of China and the terracotta army; tracked elephants in Kenya and climbed Uluru (Ayers Rock) in the middle of Australia when it was allowed. I have watched the sun rise in Sri Lanka, lunched in Hemingway's bar in Havana and there's still plenty left on my 'to do' list. I have been extremely fortunate to live when I have and to have had all the opportunities I have had. I am a different person as a result.

But travel doesn't come without risks, as Jesus, Paul and those before them certainly found. Coming home to find we'd been burgled, or getting ill while away, sometimes made me wonder if it might have been better to stay at home. For years I spent much of my time on holiday worrying about the life I'd left behind. Many people do. 'Home is where the heart is' and many don't enjoy being away from it. And that's not counting the seriously risky challenges that are way outside my own experience.

Human life often feels easier without the risk of discovery, but it cannot be what is best for us. How sad then that we have turned the Bible into something that sits on a shelf or which can never be allowed to reveal something new about ourselves that we didn't know before. How tragic that so many lives, (and, I have to say, so many churches), are stuck where they have always been and that 'newness' is often seen as something to be afraid of and resisted.

Sometimes however, change is thrust upon us whether we like it or not, like Paul's crisis of faith and conscience on the road to Damascus. We may have no choice but to move on. It may be the breakdown of a relationship or the loss of a job. It may be a change of a more subtle kind, like a realisation that we can no longer live our life as it was with integrity. A dramatic move may be required. To go on living with ourselves, we may even have to stop living with someone else. The traditional Christian teaching that people have a duty to stay where they are, even if their relationships are damaging and dehumanising, is seriously misguided. That sounds much more like the rules of the old covenant again. Travelling on may be essential for love to prevail.

Biblical people tended to travel light. They were ready for change and took the opportunity when it came. The Israelites in Egypt packed up and left when the moment came, with little or no notice and with no idea where they were going. The disciples left their nets to follow Jesus we are told, and probably left a good deal more besides, like homes, wives and children. That is a serious difficulty for people like us.

When I was a student, I could pack my worldly goods into a trunk. By the time I moved house in my forties, it took two vans. Today's younger people are at the van stage already. They'll need a fleet of lorries when they're older! We are obsessed with 'stuff'! But after a while it all starts to hold us back, to dominate our time and attention. Then moving on becomes too difficult; we have too much to lose.

Much of the feedback I have received from my first two books has been from people who, like me, used to believe something, but now cannot do so, at least in the conventional sense. They identify with the spiritual journey, but the Christian map no longer helps. Their decision has sometimes been a painful one; much that was precious had to be left behind, sometimes even very special fellow-travellers. That has been my own experience too. Perhaps it would have been easier just to have stayed where we were and faked it. I genuinely wonder how many good people are still doing that because they feel that's all they can do, not because it really 'works' for them anymore.

The comments that mean the most to me are from those who are happy to affirm that they still believe, but that perhaps they now believe in a slightly different way. More creatively; more openly and experimentally;

more bravely. The road has taken them to some new and unexpected places and they are grateful for the opportunity. But questioning our faith is hard. So is recognising the fact that we may even have to reject it and live with the consequences.

The religious quest is often presented as a journey towards ever greater certainty. I am clear that the longer I live the less I know for sure, but the more I have to reflect upon. My experience bank is well-stocked with virtual air-miles, but it has also led me to many places that have required me to think again and change direction. I'm not sure that conventional faith always does that. It often seems to be more about reassurance than reassessment. The most popular forms of religion appear to be those that simply reinforce what the believer already believes and encourage them to hold fast to it. That sounds, to me at least, like a recipe for stagnation, not for moving on.

It may be thought that I am lost because I no longer have a God to hold onto. I beg to differ. We will frequently have been told that doubt is a sin, or that a lack of faith is a sign of personal weakness. We may worry about what it will be like to let go – always a difficult thing to do – and about what life would be like on the other side. We may be afraid of what people will think of us if we begin to question what others take for granted.

But in the end we may have no choice if we are not to become far less than the person we have the capacity to be. You cannot stand still. Going nowhere is not an option. It's a bit like riding a bicycle; you have to keep pedalling or you fall off. But once you've mastered the technique, it lasts a lifetime. The journey must go on, wherever it leads. And if the map doesn't go there yet, we'll just have to update it on the way. One more (particularly wobbly) stone and we'll be back to explore that idea a bit further.

10 DREAMS AND VISIONS

A few of the Bible writers recorded their own or other people's dreams and visions: from Joseph's adventures at the beginning to John's Revelation at the end, though apart from John they are mostly in the Old Testament. These were all, in my view of course, normal dreams and individual visionary moments, not any kind of communication from an external God. It is entirely understandable that ancient people felt that they had made contact with their God in this way, but we know that dreams come from inside our brains, and our visions and hopes are part of what it means to be alive. They are not some kind of spooky film being run before our eyes by a God who is secretly trying to tell us something.

I have never entirely understood Sigmund Freud, but I am sure from my own experience that dreams somehow mop up our memories at a subconscious level and churn them out again; from 'day residues' through to information stored away that may have been untouched for years. They probably do have something to do with sex, hormones and unexpressed emotions that have been a part of us since childhood, but let's not go there now!

They also often arise from our current anxieties and the things we have been thinking about more consciously, if presented in a distorted and rather jumbled way. I have been known to wake up laughing from a dream, and sometimes the opposite. They are certainly potentially powerful and may reach down to the very centre of who we are. But in a modern world view, dreams are a routine physiological or electrical activity that can be monitored and measured externally, not any kind of inexplicable supernatural encounter.

Perhaps dreams are necessary to avoid information overload. But they often lead to new ideas and new plans of action once we wake up. Much of this book has first been written in the haze of half-sleep when a new idea has come to me in a dream that just has to be written down. I have even been known to get up and write there and then. I have obviously been thinking about it while I'm asleep, even if I wasn't aware at the time that I was doing so.

That is often also discernable as the context for the dreams that were said to have come to people in biblical times. I don't believe they were any different; their dreams grew out of what was happening to them at the time just as mine do. Joseph's dreams in Egypt arose out of what was going on around him and gave him a solution to the nation's risk of famine; that's the whole point of the story. The boy Samuel awoke to a new sense of future purpose as a man, at a time in his young life when the direction was not clear. The wise men are said to have dreamed not to go back to Herod, perhaps suspicious of his motives after their first meeting. Dreams make at least some sense, at least some of the time.

Visions are a little more complicated. In anywhere except a church, if someone came up to us and said they had seen a vision, we would probably call for a doctor. What is the difference between a 'vision' and an hallucination, fantasy or delusion? This is certainly rather more dangerous territory. Several years ago I spent a very brief time as an in-patient in a psychiatric ward. Over those few days, numerous people told me of their visions – some of them fellow-patients! They had 'seen' the Angel Gabriel anointing them (or even me) as the next Messiah; or blood coming out of the taps to drown us and the grass outside growing through the windows to choke us in our beds. These sound rather like passages from the Old Testament, but this is all madness and we help no-one by not saying so.

Sadly, nearly all of them carried Bibles, often open at the last book. I wasn't sure whether to go down this particular road here, but it seems to have forced its way in. Much of the imagery in Revelation is so bizarre as to be frightening and I prefer to stay away from it. An obsessive interest is undoubtedly unhealthy. Revelation is a particular style of 'apocalyptic' writing, of which there are other examples from the ancient world, designed to be secret and obscure for only the chosen few to understand. It purports to come direct from God. I am really not at all convinced at this point in particular.

Take it all as some kind of futuristic message from beyond and you have stepped over a line which leads to seeing the significance of 666 in someone's phone number or devil-inspired subliminal messages in the albums of rock artists. Interpreting it within its own time is an essential safeguard. Maybe there is a hidden reference to the Emperor Nero, though that is now disputed by some scholars. It is clearly aiming to point the finger at the Roman state but without making it too obvious. But stretch it to predictions about contemporary events or figures and this may not be madness, but it is certainly undesirable and extremely dangerous in the wrong hands. It merely feeds the delusions of those who are really not well enough to handle it.

Revelation's actual context reveals what Karen Armstrong calls the 'bitterness' of Johannine Christianity. We assume that the Bible writers all agreed with each other. But there was a massive argument going on at the time between those who wanted to keep the Jesus sect within mainstream Judaism and those who saw it as a radical alternative, based on a dualistic world view in which a cosmic battle was being fought between good and evil. This was John's view. As well as possible psychological factors arising from his enforced isolation, his 'visions' are grounded in fear; of the Romans, of other believers, even of his God and of the imminent end of the world. Religion based on fear is, literally, a terrible thing.

There were those who argued that Revelation should not be included in the scriptural canon and I personally rather wish they had won the day. On the other hand, I have always found it amusing when people quote from it as 'proof' that something is about to happen in our time, because 'it says in the Bible that it will be soon' – quietly ignoring the 2000 year gap since it was written! It's been 'soon' for an awfully long time. This all risks turning faith into little more than a fairground sideshow.

My interest in the Bible's dreamers and visionaries is that their dreams made a difference to their actions and their visions gave them a hope for the future, not a sense of imminent destruction. We now use both 'dream' and 'vision' in this essentially practical way to mean virtually the same as each other. When Martin Luther King said that he had a dream for the future of black Americans, he did not mean that the hope had come to him while he was asleep. For him, and for many others, to have a dream was to have a vision and a motivation for getting there. When we talk about people of vision, we don't mean that they are seeing things. We mean that they can look beyond the present and help the rest of us to see how things might be, not just how they are.

So, for example, Jesus of Nazareth had dreams and visions, not in any supernatural sense I would say, but more in line with our modern understanding of the words. He had a dream for the rule of his God on earth in which things would be done in a very different way. He had a vision and purpose for his own life, and perhaps even for his death, that would help to bring it about. That's why I am still drawn to him, even if I cannot affirm the theology that has been built upon him. That's a good way to live; a fully human way to live.

We need dreamers and visionaries more than ever. The political mantra of 'there is no alternative' seems to have become fixed and indisputable. Of course there is always an alternative; we just don't choose to take it, for whatever reason. There is always a danger that we settle for the safe, for what is; when true human fulfilment seems to require us to push the boat out and do something that goes beyond where we are and gives us a glimpse of where we might be.

We don't have to risk destroying our planet and the dreams and visions of those who can offer us another way to live should always be listened to. We don't have to settle for a third-class care system for our elderly people; we could abandon our costly nuclear weapons and beat our swords into ploughshares as a bold and visionary statement which I personally believe that others would then follow because they can't afford them either. We don't have to leave people feeling unwanted and deskilled on the dole; the vision of full-employment is just not the one we currently choose to prioritise.

It seems to me that the Biblical dreamers, perhaps leaving John the Divine aside for now, usually had alternatives. I suppose Joseph could have kept quiet about his dreams and not risked being thought of as getting 'above himself'. Samuel could have ignored the persistent voice in his sleep telling him it was time to grow up and move on. Jesus of Nazareth could have walked away from Gethsemane. I could have kept these rather unconventional understandings of spirituality to myself or even gone on saying that I believed in a God when I didn't.

It sounds a bit cheesy, but in the end you have to pursue your own dream and seek to make your own vision a reality. Only we can make a difference and if we always do what we have always done, we will always get what we have always had. We will constantly need people to stand up and give us a hope of something new and a way to find it. They must be people of integrity. Dreams and visions have to be tested; they can be 'vain'. But as it says in at least some translations of Proverbs 29 v.18: 'Where there is no vision, the people perish'. Amen to that.

CONCLUSION: UPDATING THE MAP

So, time finally to reflect on the Bible as a whole rather than on one particular aspect of it. The Bible still seems to open us up to intelligent reflection on how we live today, or at least it looks as though it has the potential to do so if we're willing to put it to work in a new way. We can address the God problem by focusing more on discovering 'His' kingdom on earth and seeking a greater understanding of our inner selves. We can address the church problem by finding enough common points of reference to enable us to walk through life together and getting on with all that needs to be done, even if we can't all believe the same things. But is this view of the Bible just a strategic device with no genuine basis?

I accept that this way of leaving the Bible behind, but also letting it spur us on to new thinking in our own time, will not be something with which everyone is comfortable. It may seem that I am writing my own Bible, not reading the one that is there already. So, here's a test. Which of the following statements are not anywhere in the Bible?

Planet Earth was created about 4004 BC.

Jonah was swallowed by a whale.

Jesus was born in a stable (and on December 25th).

Three kings came to worship him.

Mary was always a virgin.

Money is the root of all evil.

Christians should keep Sundays like the Jews keep the Sabbath.

Jesus was a handsome man with lovely blue eyes.

God is an old man with a long white beard, sitting in the sky.

The answer, of course, is that none of them are there, not just the last two, though plenty of people throughout history have believed them all. Some are admittedly almost right. It was, for example, a 'fish' that was said to have swallowed Jonah; no 'stable' is mentioned in the birth stories, only a manger and it's 'the love' of money that is the root of all evil according to 1 Timothy 6 v.10, not money itself. But, just to make the point, none of them are exactly right. Some are just opinion; some are genuine beliefs, but not biblical. Even so, the Bible might be claimed as the source for them all. How, for example, did classical artists decide how to portray Jesus? The only (possible) description we have in ancient literature is not very flattering and the Gospels are entirely silent on the issue. But the images tend to have a remarkable consistency which has effectively created a 'truth' that is often just taken for granted.

There is a danger that we can all create the Bible (or the Jesus) that we want and make the texts say what we want them to say. But 'it ain't necessarily so'. In this Conclusion, I want to consider more global questions about whether most people of faith, and no doubt many others, have got the Bible all wrong, and not just by assuming things are there which actually aren't. Forgive me if that sounds rather self-opinionated given the Bible's status, but several important issues come to mind.

Where did the idea come from that a book, or a set of books, should have so much authority? How did words clearly written by men, (inevitably only men!), become the inerrant 'Word of God', and what exactly is lost, or better still gained, when you ditch the very suggestion? Might we even be able to imagine living well without it and does a different kind of spirituality necessarily have to be 'scriptural' at all? Can we reach new understandings that hadn't been thought of when it was written and create, as it were, a new map for a new journey that goes beyond where they had reached by then?

There is very little in the Bible itself which can point to its own final authority. The text usually quoted is 2 Timothy 3 v.16. Paul writes that 'all scripture is inspired by God', but we don't know what writings he was specifically referring to. It can only have been from what we call the Old Testament and certainly didn't include his own letters. And his claim here is only that the writings are 'profitable' or 'useful', not the last word on everything for ever. There are other references that can be used here and there but nearly all of them again speak of the primacy of the Old Testament writings, which Christians effectively reject or re-interpret anyway.

The survival and growth of Christianity in our part of the world, and in many others, was largely down to sociological and political influences, not to the Bible, so let's be honest and say so. The Bible wasn't actually all that important. From Emperor Constantine onwards, whole nations became 'Christian' without knowing anything about what they'd been signed up to. It was a process of imperial expansion that kept the faith alive, not any kind of evangelistic campaign and personal commitment by those who believed the story for themselves. The life of the church was a very human business; much more about structures, authority and power than about individuals accepting for themselves what the Bible actually said. Most didn't know what it said, only what they were told.

For the first 1400 years of the Christian era there was no Bible, not at least one that anyone read outside the monasteries. Everything was still on parchments, being copied out by scribes for extremely limited circulation. Thousands upon thousands of Christians lived and died without even being aware of it, let alone being able to read it. Other forms of communication, such as the visual drama of the Mass, or the painted walls of churches and Cathedrals, were much more important as a way of sharing what they were supposed to believe.

It is very hard even to imagine what it meant to 'believe' throughout that time. Certainly not what faith is said to be all about today; a concept anything like 'a personal relationship with God/Jesus' would have been totally alien, except for the privileged few who devoted their lives to prayer, writing and study. Christianity was the accepted intellectual and moral backdrop to life, not a conscious lifestyle choice. The Bible was just another part of it, but mostly it was outside people's direct experience.

It seems that it was Jewish scholars who first started to examine what the scriptures were and what they actually said, during the early part of the second millennium. They had a vested interest of course; they wanted to challenge the claims that Christians were making. So they questioned the way their ancient texts had been used. They were not about Jesus at all, but arose from situations that belonged to their own time. The 'Servant Songs' in Isaiah; the supposed prediction of a 'virgin birth'; the Messianic claims that Christians made, all came under scrutiny. The texts themselves simply did not support such convictions; it was all a question of <u>later</u> interpretation. Christians had understood the Bible for their own purposes – as any human movement would – not remained true to the 'original'.

Then there were those who began to argue that what might at first appear to be fact could equally be seen as hyperbole or metaphor: 'This is my body', for example; it's a complex image about the enduring presence of Jesus for the believer, not a statement about human biology or the physical constitution of a wafer. Others challenged the excessive anthropomorphism that had given God what were clearly human characteristics. God cannot have literally 'walked' in the Garden of Eden, (or I would say equally literally have 'sent his Son').

For the first time the Bible was taken down from its pedestal and measured against what else we know to be true. I wish I'd met Maimonides (1135-1204). He wrote a book called 'The Guide of the Perplexed' – my kind of theologian! Others pointed out the inconsistencies between the various writers and the futility of attempts to harmonise the different versions of events into one, even in the Gospels. All this meant that simplistic statements about the whole Bible's unfailing accuracy could be given very little credence and few, if any, took up such a position. The early church conferences were full of debate; for example, about the meaning of individual words and over how much could be seen as allegory.

I suppose it was Martin Luther and the later reformers who put the Bible at the centre, at least as far as Protestants are concerned. Having re-discovered the power of the written word, he was looking for ammunition to fire at what had become a corrupt church full of dubious practices, such as the selling of 'indulgences'. These gave a guarantee of eternal forgiveness, at a price. (We are back to an entirely explicable marketing strategy; not necessarily anything to do with God at all).

People were scared stiff for their own or for their ancestors' souls in the face of an increasingly lurid portrayal of eternal torment, which has scarcely any significant basis in the Bible itself. Artists have a lot to answer for again here! But having created a sense of moral panic, the problem then required a solution, so the church came up with an extremely lucrative one. The fact that we have seen through this somewhat cynical process, and others much like it in more modern times, lies behind much of our contemporary scepticism.

But if it came down to a choice between the failings of a human institution and the 'inspired' guidance of the scriptures, the reformers judged that the Bible must take precedence, completely overlooking the fact that it too was the product of human minds with particular reasons for writing as they did at the time. The church could not claim to be above reproach, but the Bible must be. As more and more people were able to read, and with the invention of mass printing, in English and in other vernacular languages, the way was then open for a new emphasis on the Bible as the source of all truth.

'*Sola scriptura*' became the focus: 'scripture alone' could show the way. Most contemporary debate about the Bible, such as there is one, goes back to whether or not this has been the last word on the issue. The insights of 19th and 20th century historical and textual scholarship in particular have often been overlooked, or judged too difficult and challenging for 'ordinary' believers to cope with. As a result, the Bible has often had two distinct lives; one in the churches and an entirely different one in universities. I still remember the more earnest students on my theology degree course suggesting that lectures and seminars should begin with prayer for 'guidance', just in case anyone was tempted to put forward an opinion of their own. This did not go down well with their academic tutors!

Views about the Bible have now become entrenched and increasingly polarised. The fundamentalist 'right', especially in parts of Africa and the USA, still wants to claim the supremacy of the Bible in all things, and in ever-louder voices. But it is often clearly interpreted to suit certain moral, social and political ends, including, for example, a claim that the Bible exposes a global conspiracy of evil through the activities of the United Nations! Saying such things with stridency does not make them true. Winston Churchill used to write in the margins of his speeches, if he knew the point was weak, 'shout here'!

To me this, as much as anything, is an abuse of the Bible; worse than anything a non-believer can do by ignoring it. We are back to the worst excesses of pre-Reformation times in which human motives were dressed up as 'God's will' – an extremely dangerous concept. The worry is that one day someone might just get elected USA president on such a 'Bible-based' manifesto, as several candidates have promised in advance. Such a world would be a nightmare for rational people to live in. And of course, not only Christians espouse extreme views like these or claim authority for their actions from their scriptures.

Thankfully, on this side of the Atlantic we are generally nothing like so bothered. There is still a strong tradition of literary analysis of the Bible in many parts of mainland Europe, while in the UK we have settled for a traditional British fudge. We know it's got a human history, but it doesn't really make any difference to how we read it. A few people try to hang onto the idea of the Bible's inerrancy, but most believers pick and choose the bits they like and ignore the rest.

Take, for example, the never-ending debate about how the Church of England should respond to the obvious fact that some people are both gay and Christian or whether women can be bishops. It often comes down to a discussion about whether or not we are still tied to the views of St. Paul. Either 'that was then and this is now' or what he said counts for all time. Or we just argue what we think is right and then look for the texts to back us up! This all strikes me as extremely sterile.

My own view is that once we accept that humans wrote the Bible, humans can change the way we use it. We always have done; but we must be honest and acknowledge that it is all our own doing. The various books in the Bible have always been a living, evolving thing; first over the centuries as they were being written and then over even more centuries as they were edited, interpreted and used. They are a rolling record of human religious activity at the time, not the unchangeable source of it, then or now.

The reality of religion comes from us and from our experience of seeking answers to questions in our own lives, not from an ancient book with pseudo-magical powers. It must operate in the here and now and in ever-changing contexts. The idea that any truth can be fixed forever 2000, 1000 or 500 years ago is against everything else we know about life. The important thing is that we each make our own decisions about how to live well, not just try to borrow someone else's conclusions from the past. It's our spirituality that should be the focus, not theirs.

Maybe the Bible is a bit like an out-of-date sat nav! The general direction of travel is still the same – finding the best way to live and a personal sense of wellbeing and meaning. Previous travellers have found it useful before us, but we have now gone beyond the boundaries of its pre-programmed map. The Bible's writings may have made sense at the time, (though they weren't by any means the only directions on offer even then), but they didn't tell the whole story and forever.

Try to follow it all to the letter and you will soon lose your way. It now sends us along old roads that aren't there anymore because we've closed or upgraded them in the light of what we have discovered since. Other roads are entirely missing because they weren't built then. The route offered by conventional faith and its scriptures no longer fits with what many of us can see out of the car windows!

The Bible cannot be exempt from the process of making new discoveries about ourselves. It is part of our story; for some a very important part, but not on a different plane from everything else we have ever said and done. As long as we go on living as a species; as long as we each have to face up to what it means to be human, I cannot see how a book, frozen in its time and from such a narrow spectrum of our collective experience, can be given more than its fair share of attention as an unchangeable guide to the present. It has always had to be rewritten for a new audience. The important thing is that we do it with integrity, not try to claim that it is something it isn't.

So, let's treat it like any other historical source; useful, instructive; a glimpse into our collective past and still well worth a look. I would be less than the person I hope to be if I do not treat the Bible with respect. Others have walked across this river before me and the ancient stones still bear witness to where they found something secure to stand on. They point the way. I can even see the dents where they put their feet. But, of course, it is not the same river as it was then. We have known since Heraclitus (c.540-480 BC) that 'all things flow'. Rivers are a metaphor for life, history, religion, everything.

And just as the river is constantly changing, so are we. A little way downstream we have built a spanking new footbridge based on all the latest technology and scientific understanding that wasn't there before. That doesn't mean we should now rip the stones up, but pretending that the bridge doesn't exist, or still relying on an old map that doesn't show it, is just not possible. Surely the modern bridge can also get us to where we need to go, just as those who laid the stones originally intended?

They might even think that we've improved the route and done the best we can in our time, just as they did in theirs. Until, that is, future bridge-builders come up with an even better crossing and an even more sophisticated map. Our legacy to those who come after us can only be where we have got to so far, but then, just like us, it's up to them what they do with it.

BY THE SAME AUTHOR

WALKING WITHOUT GOD
In Search of a Humanist Spirituality

In these nine short essays, together with an extended introduction, Ben Whitney uses verses from the Psalms to explore some of the big questions that religions are about. If you take a God out of the equation, what are you left with?

FINDING THE WAY
Parables for a Secular Pilgrim

Characters such as the Good Samaritan are written deep into our secular culture and values. So is Jesus still worth following, even if you cannot believe in the religion built around him?

£4.99 EACH FROM
www.ypd-books.com